SURRENDER

SURRENDER

LARRY B. REESE

For additional copies, visit:
www.lulu.com

Cover and Interior Design by Greer Wymond | www.thecreativebird.com

Edited by Karin Robertson

ISBN: 978-1-105-99062-5

Scripture quotations are taken from:
The Amplified Bible, Expanded Edition
Copyright © 1987 by the Zondervan Corporation and the Lockman Foundation.

For my students.
~ LARRY B. REESE

SURRENDER

Foreword

Time is a great revealer. The weakness or strength of most things comes to the surface over time. Most especially is this true in the lives of people. A person may "fake it" for a short time, but eventually, the truth, i.e., the character of a person, is revealed. Time is exactly what I have had with the author of this book on "surrender." Larry Reese and I have had the time needed to know each other well. With well over twenty years of working together, walking together, and warring together, I have come to know the true character of Larry Reese and his ministry.

For a book to be of any lasting benefit to its reader, its author should have walked out and practically applied its content. No surgical student would want to study a textbook written by a person who had only read and repeated what he had read from another textbook. Theory is necessary, but when I read a book, I want the author to have learned by practice the theory behind the principles.

Larry Reese is such a man. I watched him leave his home in Alabama and move to North Carolina to join our ministry team there. I saw his surrender to leave and move to Georgia when the team moved to Tennessee. I watched as he laid aside his school and planted a church all because the King asked it of him. I saw him leave the church he planted and wait on the Lord's next move because he asked him to. I prayed with him while he surrendered his home, friends and family to move to Ohio to be part of someone else's vision, simply because he is surrendered to his Master. Yes! I want to know that the one, who purports to teach me, has something to say. I say yet again, Larry Reese is such a man.

This is a book about "surrender." It is not a hard concept to understand at all. One simply gives up possessions or person into the authority of another, while relinquishing one's power, aims and goals. No, it is not a hard thing to understand. However, the step from understanding to undertaking is a giant leap. Let my friend and brother help you take that step in his work: *Surrender.*

Many centuries ago, the Bishop of Hippo, Augustine, in his pre-conversion days, heard children in the street saying, "take and read, take and read." Finding his scripture opened to the Book of Romans chapter fourteen, he began to read and before he was finished, he had given his life to the Lord Jesus Christ. If you listen closely, you can hear the chant of the children in the street saying, "take and read, take and read."

Take and Read
Frank A. McCarley
President and Founder
Malachi Ministries International, Inc.
Living Stones Global University

I

Surrender

"...On the left hand [and to the north] where He works [I seek Him],
but I cannot behold Him; He turns Himself to the right hand [and
to the south], but I cannot see Him. But He knows the way that
I take [He has concern for it, appreciates, and pays attention to
it]. When He has tried me, I shall come forth as refined gold [pure
and luminous]." JOB 23:9–10

All of us are creatures of habit. We want to control what comes into our lives as much as we possibly can. However, there are certain things that we cannot control and have no control over. Oftentimes as Christians we say that we believe that our heavenly Father is in control of our lives, but when it comes to pain, hurt, and difficult situations, we often wonder where God is and why He has allowed adversity in our lives. Truth be told, difficulty is always around us—sometimes we are successful in avoiding it, but as we continue to move along in life, eventually something will happen in our lives that is well beyond our control.

As we look at and examine our opening Scripture from Job, we see a man who has been through great difficulty, not really understanding his circumstances. We know the story of Job: how the Father allowed Satan to take practically everything he had, including causing him to experience terrible and painful body sores, but we often fail to learn from the story what we should. So many times we see difficulty in the lives of our friends and family members and those we consider good people, and find it terribly difficult to understand why certain good people suffer and go through difficulty. This is not necessarily a book about why bad things happen to good people, but a look at what happens in all of our lives in the form of suffering, and what we should do with that suffering when it comes. We are told well by Jesus:

> *"...I have told you these things, so that in me you may have [perfect] peace and confidence. In the world you have tribulation and trials and distress and frustration; but be of good cheer [take courage; be confident, certain, undaunted]! For I have overcome the world. [I have deprived it of power to harm you and have conquered it for you.]* JOHN 16:33

Jesus is not suggesting that we look forward to suffering and difficult times. He is simply saying that these types of circumstances come into our lives because we are living in this world. Our success, according to Jesus, isn't through financial security or other methods we engage in to avoid hardship, it comes from looking to Him. We look at how Jesus lived in this world without being controlled by it. In this life difficulty, stress, death of a loved one, sickness, and disease are unavoidable. We must have an intimate knowledge of Who Jesus is and how He lived victoriously in this world so we can do the same. It is very important to understand that when we are born again, we become a brand new creation as far as God is concerned. We become like newborns. Let us remember that when a baby is born, he/she has no past to be concerned with. Just as a newborn craves milk to survive, we must develop a spiritual diet from our heavenly Father that sustains us and gives us the ability to walk in this world in spiritual power. This new diet consists of everything we need as born again Christians—first we drink milk and then we grow up and eat a meatier diet as our spiritual senses mature in Christ Jesus. This maturity in Christ allows us to better understand and know God. It is also wise to understand that God speaks to us as His children. Once we are born again, we are restored to "first rights" with Him. This means that we were once alienated and estranged from Him because of our sins, but we are now able to speak with Him personally and intimately. We can hear Him share His heart and thoughts, which causes the Scriptures that we study to make sense. Another way of saying this is that God's thoughts in Scripture begin to come alive to us. Through rebirth, we now have the mind of God and can think as He thinks. This is a process, dear ones, that comes over time—it cannot be rushed or forced. Since our Father is in charge of this new relationship, He will instruct us and give us insight into Himself so that we will better know who we are. Chiefly, we cannot know who we are if we do not know Who our heavenly Father is. We may have an idea of what we would like to be, go after it with all of our hearts, and maybe even accomplish it. However, without the knowledge of the holy developing within us, we cannot know who we are from God's perspective. This lack of intimate knowledge and insight hinders our progress even in this world. We must understand that it is not the desire for wealth and fame that should compel us forward, but the desire to know Jesus as our Savior and First Born Brother from the dead. When I say First Born Brother from the dead, I am saying that Jesus lived and breathed the exact way that we do and learned how to live above what we often live underneath. This is why He was able to say 'I have overcome the world.'

For a moment, let us look at Job again. I particularly want to mention two times when we see that Job was afraid. We'll look at how reverential fear and ungodly fear affected him as well as it affects us.

> *"...There was a man in the land of Uz whose name was Job; and that man was blameless and upright, and one who [reverently] feared God and abstained from and shunned evil [because it was wrong]."* JOB 1:1

We must consider that Job was made right in God's eyes because he shunned and abstained from evil. Because Job spent time with God he knew that evil was wrong. Dear ones, if we are in true fellowship with the Father, then we seldom worry about sinning or the consequences that come from sin. The blood of Jesus that has been shed for us consummating the covenant has given us clear consciences so that we are no longer tormented by the thoughts of sin. However, if we do not remain in innocent fellowship with the Father, then the thoughts of sin will continue to torment us, keeping and maintaining ground within our hearts where Jesus' righteousness should be reigning instead. When I say the righteousness of Jesus, I mean the things that kept Jesus in intimate fellowship with the Father which enabled Him to do His Father's will. Jesus was consumed with doing His Father's will, but not out of obligation, religious duty, or fear. Jesus obeyed the Father because He (knew) His Father and had an intimate relationship with Him. Jesus loved Him. Believe me when I tell you, Jesus knows how much His Father loves us because of how much He loves Him. Like Jesus, we are able to have the same type of intimate relationship with the Father.

This passage in Job says that Job reverently feared God. This reverential fear is the kind of fear that the Father wants us to have because it gives us insight and clarity into the Person of God, enabling us to know God as He reveals Himself. We must remember that being good does not equate righteousness because if we are being good in our own strength, then righteousness is somewhere underneath our efforts to be good. We must understand that the presence of righteousness in us through Jesus Christ rids us of the obligatory feelings we have to be good. We must also observe here that if we are trying to be good then we will also, even if unconsciously, try to win blessings and favor from God out of our own efforts, rather than out of the completion of the work on the cross that is now alive in us by the Holy Spirit's power. To fear the Lord the way that Job did in Chapter One means that through this kind of respectful fear of the Lord, Job gained insight into the Person of God the Father and learned from spiritual observation how to obey Him. When I say spiritual observation, I mean that Job was able to 'see' what God was doing in him and how to obey Him. As we learn to obey God and to respectfully fear Him, the easier it will be to recognize Him and His ways. This revelation of God's ways comes from being taught by an inner witness by the Holy Spirit. Therefore, we do what the Father wants us to do and our consciences remain clear. We no longer have to struggle with condemning thoughts from Satan. We are able to move along freely in life, walking with God, without struggling with constant harassing thoughts from Satan, telling us that we are no good. This is where we come to the second fear that Job spoke about in Chapter Three.

> *"...For my sighing comes before my food, and my groanings are poured out like water. For the thing which I greatly fear comes upon me, and that of which I am afraid befalls me. I was not or am not at ease, nor had I or have I rest, nor as I or am I quiet, yet trouble came and still comes upon me."* **JOB 3:24,25,26**

We must pay careful attention to the words of Scripture—they mean something. Oftentimes we want to skip over the difficult parts and the passages that speak about suffering and hurting, but the Father has those passages in the Bible for a reason. As we look at Job, we already know that he was a man who did not take to evil very kindly. He did all the right things, or the things that many of us would associate with making him a good person, and then all of a sudden this great calamity comes upon him from Satan. It is essential that we realize that Job was a threat to Satan because of his obedience to our Father. Without operating in faith, it is impossible to please God and to feel the Father's pleasure with us, so not operating in faith pretty much causes Satan to remain at bay from us; however, when we begin to move forward in our walk with God, having faith in His word, it causes a spiritual chemical reaction in Satan's kingdom. In other words, the kingdom of darkness knows that something is happening in someone who is trying to break free from areas where Satan has held him or her captive. It is through the spiritual insight of the Holy Spirit that we recognize that Jesus has paid the ransom for us and we no longer belong to Satan. We now belong to the One Who has purchased us, but Satan takes advantage of this by causing us to be afraid or to keep us believing that we cannot wholly approach God because of some remaining sinful habit or sin in general. As long as we believe that this is true and that there is something keeping us from God, then we will feel that our Father is distant from us.

If we look at Job's actions in Chapter One and following, we see that fear was a factor in his life. It wasn't that he was doing the wrong things, but Satan took advantage of what he was doing right and made something wrong out of it because Job was operating out of fear to some degree. Fear that is motivated by dread or the fear of what might happen if we do not do everything just right, gives Satan a doorway through which he can actually petition God for us. Fear weakens our faith, and Job was placing some of his faith in what he was afraid of that might happen. Here in Chapter Three he says, "what I have feared the most has come upon me." He was literally afraid that this calamity or destruction of some kind could come upon him because he said it. Now dear ones, it is important that we recognize and learn something from this. Sometimes it doesn't matter that we cross all the T's and dot all the I's, difficult things will happen in this life and not necessarily directly because of our disobedience to God, but because difficult things happen period. The important thing is that when these things happen to us, we recognize them through the eyes of faith in Christ Jesus and not through the eyes of tormenting fear. We must also understand that fear also brings about the spirit of not knowing what is happening, leaving us perplexed, and wondering where the Father is in all of this trouble. However, having a determined and steadfast faith in the Father allows us to have peace in whatever situation we are in, giving us the spiritual patience we need to wait on Him for an answer.

Let us see clearly that Satan takes advantage of us wherever fear and blame can be found in our relationship with God our Father. Satan wants us to find fault in God when difficult things happen, so that we may accuse the Father the way that Satan accuses the Father and us as His children. Remember, dear ones, that having faith in Jesus Christ allows us to recognize where our shortcomings are without the condemnation that can come from those things being revealed to us. Jesus always shows us the way out—even if it doesn't come in the form of physical escape, but as a promise of coming through the test or trial. However, Satan looks for opportunities to harm us, to show us hate, difficulty, and even in the times when our faith may not be strong enough, to blame God for something that Satan may actually be doing himself.

"...Be well balanced (temperate, sober of mind), be vigilant and cautious at all times; for that enemy of yours, the devil, roams around like a lion roaring [in fierce hunger], seeking someone to seize upon and devour. Withstand him; be firm in faith [against his onset—rooted, established, strong, immovable, and determined], knowing that the same (identical) sufferings are appointed to your brotherhood (the whole body of Christians) throughout the world." **1 PETER 5:8,9**

2

Thinking the Right Way

"...But the Lord God called to Adam and said to him, Where are you? He said, I heard the sound of You [walking] in the garden, and I was afraid because I was naked; and I hid myself. And He said, Who told you that you were naked? Have you eaten of the tree of which I commanded you that you should not eat?"
GENESIS 3:9,10,11

One of the ways we know that we are communing with God is when we readily seek Him or when He draws us into His Presence. As we obey our Father, the Holy Spirit reveals God's thoughts to us so that we know when He is either speaking to or wanting to spend time with us. Ideally, our heavenly Father's desire is to cause us to be so familiar with Him that we run to Him whether we believe we need Him or not. Sadly, even the church has taught us, to run to God primarily only when we need something. However, our greatest times with God come when we simply sit with Him or recline upon Him with our entire beings.

When I say entire, I am speaking of releasing every care and concern that tries to force us to look elsewhere to find the rest and peace that only our Father can provide.

In our opening Scripture passage, we see that Adam ran and hid himself from the Father. This had never happened during their time of intimate fellowship, so obviously, something had happened—even the spiritual climate of the garden had changed. What once was a welcoming atmosphere for Adam and the Father to fellowship together had turned into an atmosphere of fear. In a short period of time, Adam had grown to be afraid of God.

Oftentimes, we do not understand or seek out what Adam and the Father were doing during those times of fellowship in the garden. Just as the Father was teaching Adam and Eve about Himself, He desires to do the same with us today. Because we fail to know Him intimately, we often accuse the Father of wrongdoing when we do not understand certain things. Sadly, Satan was able to get Adam and Eve off course in the impressionable days of their lives, when they were very sensitive, and desiring to know more about the Father as well as the world in which they lived. We must understand that God has created us to desire to know the truth, but not at any cost. He has provided us with the Holy Spirit, the third Person of the Trinity Who agrees with both the Father and the Son to present the Father to us in a way that we may be able to understand Him naturally.

"...The Spirit of Truth, Whom the world cannot receive (welcome, take to its heart), because it does not see Him or know and recognize Him, for He lives with you [constantly] and will be in you." JOHN 14:17

When God was walking with Adam and Eve in the garden, He taught them everything that they needed to know about Himself as well as the world they lived in. The primary danger of Adam and Eve eating from the tree of the knowledge of good and evil is that knowledge gets in the way of the truth. What we know may not necessarily always be true. When Satan lied and deceived Adam and Eve, the spirit of deception entered into their lives. This resulted in competition with the Father's voice which made it even harder for them to discern. What was once the reverential fear of the Lord turned into being afraid of God. This fear was not present before Satan lied to them.

Dear ones, as we grow the way the Father desires, we cannot help but grow in love. Faith and love will always work together and support each other. However, when fear enters the picture, something is wrong. John writes this to assure us of this truth:

"...There is no fear in love [dread does not exist], but full-grown (complete, perfect) love turns fear out of doors and expels every trace of terror! For fear brings with it the thought of punishment, and [so] he who is afraid has not reached the full maturity of love [is not yet grown into love's complete perfection]." 1 JOHN 4:18

When we operate in fear, we begin to think differently. Rather than living by faith, we allow fear to control us and cause us to believe lies about the Father. Without faith in God, we take our lives into our own hands. When we are thinking wrong thoughts about God and ourselves, we are also experiencing feelings that agree with fear rather than peace. If we are influenced by thoughts of fear, then we are enslaved by those thoughts. However, as we follow the Father's instructions through His Word, we continue to believe God and live by faith. Thus, our lives are filled with peace.

It is important that we realize that Satan causes us to be afraid. He often masquerades and disguises himself as God to trick us into questioning the Father and what He tells us. While there is nothing wrong with asking the Father questions, it is wise to listen to Him first. When we listen to God, wisdom comes into our hearts and minds. This doesn't happen as much when we speak to Him, unless our questions are based upon the wisdom that He has already established in our hearts through communion with Him. Satan is a major strategist. He desires for us to take his bait and be wounded by it. Once we begin to believe that God is not good and become suspicious of Him, our ability to have intimacy with Him is challenged by the lie that we believe. If this is the case, then Satan has truly caused us to stumble.

> *"...And the Lord God said to the woman, What is this you have done?   And the woman said, The serpent beguiled (cheated, outwitted, and deceived) me, and I ate."* GENESIS 3:13

As intimacy grows between our heavenly Father and us, we will find that Satan's ability to deceive us will diminish. We will begin to recognize the spirit behind his lies more quickly.

Also, as we mature our thinking will change. God intends for our minds to change so that we will have self-control and enjoy fellowship with Him and each other. It is through our fellowship with the Father that He reveals His intention for us being in the world.

So, why is faith so important to the Father and to us in our relationship with Him? It is having faith in God's Word that enables us to overcome the lies and deception of Satan. We learn from John:

"...For whatever is born of God is victorious over the world; and this is the victory that conquers the world, even our faith. Who is it that is victorious over [that conquers] the world but he who believes that Jesus is the Son of God [who adheres to, trusts in, and relies on that fact]?" 1 JOHN 5:4,5

We can be sure that if we are listening to the Father and believing Him, He will respond by speaking to us. The older we become in Christ, the more our faith will be tested. It is important to know that God does not tempt us. It is Satan who tries to tempt us away from our faith in God. Whenever this happens, we should always believe that our Father has our best interest at heart. We can count on Him to lead us back to Himself and restore us to the purpose that He has called us to.

As we respond quickly to the Father's voice, we see that He calls upon us more frequently. And with each encounter that we have with God, our minds are changed as we think the way that the Father intended—through faith in His words. Our Father speaks from an eternal perspective and He intentionally limits Himself to time and space because we are limited. However, through the Holy Spirit, the Father shares things with us about the future just as He said He would. He also gives us the ability to receive His words so that our faith may be strong during difficult times. Just as our heavenly Father is always communicating with us, we must believe it and look for ways He is revealing Himself. Regardless of what happens in this life, we can be ready for it with the faithfulness He has caused to arise in our hearts.

3

The Way of Faith

"...But He knows the way that I take [He has concern for it, appreciates, and pays attention to it]." JOB 23:10

When we become born again Christians, it can sometimes seem like our heavenly Father is distant or even silent. He has His reasons for everything He does. He intends for us to be aware of Who He is so that we may fully engage with Him. Out of everything that Father created, man is the only being who has His spirit. Because Father has deposited Himself within us, He pays close attention to us. When people look at us closely, they may recognize our resemblance to our earthly parents. The same thing is true about us as our Father's children. When we are born again, we begin to reveal the Father's glory and resemble His distinct characteristics. These changes take place as we seek the Father more intimately.

As we examine this Chapter's opening Scripture, we should ask ourselves why does the Father have concern for the road that each of us takes? Mostly, it is because He knows where the road leads and where He desires for us to go. Our heavenly Father has not put us in the world to fend for ourselves. He put us here at the right place and the right time so that we can get to know Him on the path that He has chosen.

We cannot find our heavenly Father through intellectual pursuit. We know Him through the revelation of Himself that only He can provide. We find our way to Him because He has already placed that path before us. He also gives us the ability to know He is behind it. We often do not recognize these simple ways that our Father reveals Himself because we are preoccupied with our own way. We seek God on our own terms. The Father is always standing in a place of mystery and revelation. He has already placed within us the desire to look for Him which cannot be found naturally. Even in nature and the wonders of creation, there is evidence that He exists. These are foundations upon which we are to further seek and find Him.

It is important to recognize once again that Satan deceived Adam and Eve through trickery and deception. Satan twisted what God had already spoken to them and made it seem all right to dishonor what He had told them. Satan wants us to believe that we should use our own discretion to decide if we want to obey what the Father says or not. My dear ones, let us recognize with all of our hearts that whenever the Father instructs us to do something, it is a command from His lips. Obeying our Father's instructions gives us freedom. Because we have lived so long in bondage to our own pursuits, we have not recognized our Father. Although we live by sight, we are told in Scripture that the just, those who have been justified by Christ Jesus and live by faith, have spiritual insight into God's divine nature. As we continue to live by faith, the Holy Spirit gives us insight and sometimes reveals the Father's plans for us. We should not live from blessing to blessing. We should recognize Christ Jesus as the ultimate blessing and pursue Him.

> "...For we are God's [own] handiwork (His workmanship), recreated in Christ Jesus, [born anew] that we may do those good works which God predestined (planned beforehand) for us [taking paths which He prepared ahead of time], that we should walk in them [living the good life which He prearranged and made ready for us to live]." EPHESIANS 2:10

When we look at this Scripture, we can clearly see that our heavenly Father plans out our lives ahead of time. He reserves His greatest plans for those who come to Him through Christ Jesus. Even though we go through difficult times, we must believe that God desires for us to have a good life in this world. There is a difference between our walking with God on the road that He has chosen and our choosing our own way. The distinction is that our Father is with us on His chosen way. He reveals Himself at the right time and reminds us of His promises so we do not give up and faint inwardly.

We often give up on the inside long before we actually manifest our outward hopelessness. God gives grace to those who humble themselves and seek His way. Sometimes we wonder if it is possible to walk the way the Father has chosen. The answer is found in our personal surrender to Him. Even when we surrender to the Father, we often struggle because we run into roadblocks.

During these times, we must remain sober minded and think the right way. We must realize that roadblocks are not meant to be the end of the journey. They are meant to point us in another direction which is the way that our Father has chosen for us.

We have discussed that right thinking is needed so that we may know the Father's will. Remember, our heavenly Father will sometimes allow or cause certain difficulties to happen so that we may stop and think. During these times, we can see from the revelation He gives us that He is involved in what we are doing. Oftentimes, when we are walking with our Father, we are not really thinking. We are allowing our feelings to instruct us rather than the message or the words that the Father is speaking to us. During the times of mental struggle, our Father is not absent. He is allowing us to look inwardly from the soul to the higher place of spiritual reasoning so that we may see the way that He has chosen.

> *"...But He knows the way that I take...He has concern for it... appreciates it..."* **JOB 23:10**

Dear ones, it is when we begin to experience trouble, frustration, doubt and fear that we either call out to God the most or seek a way to escape our discomfort. But as we see in the Scripture above, the Father knows the way that we must take. He has personally designed it, executed it, and prepared it perfectly so that we may walk in it. We will, however, continue to fight against the way He has chosen if we do not believe that God is good and we remain disobedient. We cannot know the way that the Father has chosen if we continue to walk independently of Him.

"... For I have known (chosen, acknowledged) him [as My own], so that he may teach and command his children and the sons of his house after him to keep the way of the Lord and to do what is just and righteous, so that the Lord may bring Abraham what He has promised him." GENESIS 18:19

In the Old Testament, Abraham obeyed God by leaving his home. The Father sent Abraham away from the unbelieving influences of his own family. To us this may seem harsh that our Father would require us to give up and to leave our family behind. The Father, however, is interested in faith and where faith can be found. Faith is not always found in families, but individuals. We do not often see whole families following Jesus Christ with fully engaged hearts. Our Father chooses certain people whom He knows will have faith in Him, execute His plan, and walk alongside Him. Just as the Father walked with Adam, He taught Abraham in their fellowship to walk in His ways and to teach others. Although the way of the Father is mysterious and sometimes troublesome for those who walk with Him, He does not fail to honor His words. It is impossible for the Father not to honor His word because His word represents Himself—the Person Who He actually is. Every word that our Father speaks to us in His promises is an 'oath' that He cannot and will not break.

Dear ones, as we walk along this road that our Father has chosen for us, we will learn to walk with Him without stumbling as often as we did before. We are not only hearing our Father's voice, but we are growing in the nature of God also. As God reveals Himself to us, we begin to 'see' Him more clearly. Our fear of the unknown begins to disappear because what was once hidden for us suddenly becomes clear.

> *"...We know [absolutely] that anyone born of God does not [deliberately and knowingly] practice committing sin, but the One Who was begotten of God carefully watches over and protects him [Christ's divine presence within him preserves him against the evil], and the wicked one does not lay hold (get a grip) on him or touch [him]." 1 JOHN 5:18*

The Scripture often causes fear in the hearts of believers because we still see ourselves as habitual sinners. As we get to know what the Father thinks and how He leads us in His ways, we begin to think righteously. We begin to understand that we have the mind of Christ Who is the victorious One over death, hell, and the grave, as well as all of Satan's tricks. Remember, this is a journey, dear ones, and we are to walk along the way that our Father has chosen for us so that we find our acquaintance with our elder Brother, Jesus. The more we walk the way that our Father has chosen, the more we see that we have inherited His power to live and not simply exist in this world.

4

Is God Punishing Me?

"...Even today is my complaint rebellious and bitter...I would lay my cause before Him and fill my mouth with arguments... I would learn what He would answer me, and understand what He would say to me." JOB 23:1A,4–5

"...Let no one say when he is tempted, I am tempted from God; for God is incapable of being tempted by [what is] evil and He Himself tempts no one. But every person is tempted when he is drawn away, enticed and baited by his own evil desire (lust, passions)." JAMES 1:13–14

When things go wrong in our lives, we have the natural tendency to wonder if God is punishing us. Although we want things to go well all the time, we know that things can happen that are beyond our control.

The key to victorious living is to know that when we are tempted, God is not the One tempting us. We must recognize that Satan is trying to pull us away from our walk with our heavenly Father. Jesus Christ has already established a very visible walk for us to follow. We should mimic Jesus through the power of the Holy Spirit and not by religious habit. We must grow in God's power within so we can walk with Him naturally.

Many times we are religious and live by a set of rules rather than allowing our faith in Christ Jesus to instruct us inwardly. As we learn that our Father has made us in His image and desires truth, we will stop trying to be good and maintain our relationship with the Father by keeping rules. We will begin to know His love and as our love for Him increases, we will be able to breathe freely and know that righteousness is being established in our hearts and minds such that we do not have to try so hard to be good and to please God.

Dear ones, we must realize that the presence of goodness in our lives is there because Jesus Christ's righteousness has been given to us. Once we have the revelation that we have already been made right with God because of Jesus, we will be able to enjoy the Father and rest in His goodness rather than our own efforts to be good. Anything that we feel we can do to win the Father's favor is done in vain. Christ has done everything that is necessary to please the Father as the First-Born Son back from the dead. All we need do is surrender ourselves to Christ's finished work so that we may enjoy fellowship with God.

After Satan had maliciously attacked Job, the Father became silent for a while. We must also remember that when God brought the Israelites out of Egypt, He would be silent again after performing great miracles on their behalf. This silence is not intended to punish us or cause us to be afraid. It gives us an opportunity to reflect on what the Father has done and to realize the favor we've had in certain situations because of His intervention. However, our natural tendency is to complain against God in our discomfort. When things begin to settle and there are fewer visible signs of His presence, we have the tendency to lose hope. Although signs and wonders help us to know the Father is with us, we are not to have faith in them because they do not save us. Dear ones, having faith in God our Father through the work that Jesus has done on the cross and obeying His words saves and keeps us safe from the evil one. Through obedience we grow to love Jesus more because Jesus is made visible through this cultivated relationship of obedience.

We may wonder why God wants us to focus so much on obedience? The Father wants us to obey Him so that we may see Him at work in our lives and feel the Holy Spirit's growing power and presence inside us. This growing knowledge gives us the ability to know that God is with us. When we engage with Him in prayer, we find Him quickly rather than summoning Him with flattering words. Because God wants us to worship Him in spirit and in truth, we have to know how this is done. Only God can reveal Himself in such a way where our worship becomes real. When we know that we are worshiping the Father through the revelation of Himself, we then better understand how to communicate with Him. We are worshiping the One and only true God Who reveals Himself when we truly seek Him out. There is no question that the Father reveals Himself in this developing relationship of hearing and obeying.

"...If you [really] love Me, you will keep (obey) My commands."
JOHN 14:15

Obedience is important for two reasons. First it shows us that when we obey God, He keeps His word to us. Without operating in faith, we cannot experience pleasure with God or the pleasure that settles the issues concerning whether or not we are obeying God. Obedience is a natural response to loving God.

The second reason that we should obey God is because it silences the voice of the enemy. Satan is very good at playing mind games with us. As we have learned, he is a mental strategist who has caused men to doubt God for many years and is successful at it. However, God can only be approached through faith in Christ Jesus and His work on the cross.

When we realize that our self-efforts to please God fail, Satan begins to lose his mental power over us. If Satan cannot convince us that either God is not speaking to us or He is not speaking the truth, he will then accuse us of some sin that we may struggle with. Satan knows that if he can cause our faith defenses to fail, then he can possibly make us feel that God is not pleased with us. Remember this, accusation and love do not agree.

God neither accuses nor tempts us to sin. If God's love is not present in our mental interaction with Him and accusation is, then Satan is at work. Obviously, we want to feel that our Father is pleased with us. If Satan can get us to think that God is not, then he lies and causes us to feel rather than to think. While there is nothing wrong with feeling the Father's love in our hearts, we cannot fully feel love in the midst of accusation and condemnation from Satan. However, the important thing in our thinking is that we remain subjected to God's truth so that our faith is maintained in Him as well as our love for Him. When this happens, we experience emotions that are holy. These emotions cause us to know that we are thinking the right way even when things do not look so good in our lives at the moment.

> *"...Oh, that I knew where I might find Him, that I might come even to His seat! I would lay my cause before Him and fill my mouth with arguments. I would learn what He would answer me, and understand what He would say to me. Would He plead against me with His great power? No, He would give heed to me. There the righteous [one who is upright and in right standing with God] could reason with Him; so I should be acquitted by my Judge forever." JOB 23:3–7*

If we were to read the entire book of Job, we would learn that it is not wrong to complain to God, but it is wrong to complain against Him. The Israelites often complained against God when things did not go their way in the wilderness. And let us remember that when the Father is silent, it does not mean that He is distant. When we do not know His ways, our hearts are often estranged and distant from the Father. The more we grow to know God, the more we understand His ways and find peace even when He is not speaking. When the Father isn't speaking to us, it is simply another opportunity for us to get to know Him more. For instance, if the Israelites had grown to know the Father the way that He intended, they would have respected Him and asked Him for what they needed. They would have honored Him for what He did for them. The Father reveals Himself in our wilderness just as He did with the Israelites wilderness experience. Through this revelation of Himself we see ourselves as we really are without the Father's Spirit in us. We are selfish, self-reliant, hateful, arrogant, violent, and every other ungodly thing that could be listed. However, if we obey Him, our Father is able to calm and subdue this terrible nature. In truth, man was created to have intimacy with God. We may not know it, but we are all actually looking for and searching for God. Regardless of what we call it—enlightenment, peace, or truth—we are looking to return to the One Who created us. We have to do this on His terms because God's ways are intended to be eternal. We were never meant to die, but to live with Him forever. The Father speaks and addresses what we must do to enjoy life now as well as in the future.

As described in these verses, Job was looking for God and wanting to be with the Father. He wanted to share his heart to gain understanding as to why this calamity had come upon him. When we feel as uncomfortable as Job did, let us remember that when Satan attacks this way, there has to be a reason. Rather than search diligently inwardly, we should lay ourselves before God Who knows us better than we know ourselves. Because the Father desires truth in our most inner being, He shows us what needs to be done from that perspective. Dear ones, just because Satan attacks us does not always mean that we have done something wrong, but that we could be on the verge of doing something right. Our Father knows our full potential and He is always looking to reveal this to us. However, if we remain preoccupied with what Satan is doing, we remain in a vicious emotional and mental cycle trying to figure out what we have done wrong. God doesn't want us to focus on what was done that was wrong or what we may feel is wrong at the moment, but to focus on Himself so that we may know from Him what the truth is. This kind of engaging with the Father is definitely a battle because we have grown to want to feel good and believe that if everything isn't gong just the way we want it to, then something is wrong in our relationship with God. But let us remember what the Father told the Israelites in the wilderness. It is just as true for us today in the wilderness experiences of our lives.

> *"...And you shall [earnestly] remember all the way which the Lord your God led you these forty years in the wilderness, to humble you and to prove you, to know what was in your [mind and] heart, whether you would keep His commandments or not."*
> *DEUTERONOMY 8:2*

With all of our modern technology, the advancement of society, and the culture we live in, we still have trouble simply obeying God's voice. Our Father takes us from what is familiar so that we may experience Him. In His testing of us, we sometimes rebel even more against Him and fail to know that this testing is really a form of kindness. With God we do not often see how kind He is until we have been tested. We view the Father as cruel and sometimes unloving because we do not know what He is doing and cannot trace His hand in what can sometimes seem like severe testing and trouble. However, as we continue through the struggle, maintaining the right attitude or a receptive attitude and mind toward God, He will show us why certain things have happened. We become wiser concerning Him and our human condition without Him. The Israelites grumbled against the Father constantly. They never really understood that they were still prisoners within themselves even though they were out of Egypt and no longer enslaved by the Egyptians. They had even witnessed how the Father destroyed Pharaoh's army before the Red Sea, but still they rebelled. Dear ones, let us realize that rebellion is born out of unbelief. If we do not believe God, no matter what He reveals to us outwardly, we will never stop rebelling against Him.

We must take to heart that God does not tempt us to do evil. However, He will put our faith to the test as any good teacher does so that we may see for ourselves whether we pass the test. God is not trying to fail us in the testing, but to grow our strength, knowledge, wisdom, and faith in Him so that Satan is crushed when he tries to tempt us. We see our Savior being tempted as we are, but Jesus always found the means of escape. That same means of escape is available to us, but is better recognized in continued intimacy with God. It is not wise for us to never or sparingly spend time with God and expect Him to just be there when we call. The Father is with us at all times, but if we do not listen to Him for a long time, it is harder to recognize His voice. The means of escape may not always be physical deliverance. It may be a word from God that helps us in the situation until physical deliverance occurs. It is amazing the power we have when we have a relationship with our Father and actually walk it out.

"...But God is faithful [to His Word and to His compassionate nature], and He [can be trusted] not to let you be tempted and tried and assayed beyond your ability and strength of resistance

and power to endure, but with the temptation He will [always] also provide the way out (the means of escape to a landing place), that you may be capable and strong and powerful to bear up under it patiently." 1 CORINTHIANS 10:13

"...For because He Himself [in His humanity] has suffered in being tempted (tested and tried), He is able [immediately] to run to the cry of (assist, relieve) those who are being tempted and tested and tried [and who therefore are being exposed to suffering]. HEBREWS 2:18

5

Recognizing God

"You also made a reservoir between the two walls for the water of the Old Pool, but you did not look to the Maker of it, nor did you recognize Him Who planned it long ago." **ISAIAH 22:11**

"....The sheep that are My own hear and are listening to My voice; and I know them, and they follow Me." **JOHN 10:27**

When a baby is born, the infant must know his or her mother right away without getting used to care from temporary nurses. It is important for the infant to know his or her mother's essence: the sound of her voice and the comfort of her care. The sooner the infant gets to know his or her mother, the sooner he or she relaxes and stops searching for her.

When we are born again, we come to our heavenly Father at varying stages in our lives. Since we cannot control when we are born again any more than a naturally born child, we cannot determine how long we will live by ourselves. As with the mother of a natural infant, we get to know our heavenly Father Who has given birth to us in the spiritual realm by His Holy Spirit. This is where we often struggle and fail to live victorious Christian lives. We know what we are supposed to do because of what we read in the Scriptures. However, without the Father's instructions, we continue to fall short in our ability to know Him because we do not know how to recognize our Father.

The opening passage tells us that as the sheep of Christ we know His voice. The issue is settled whether or not we can hear His voice because Jesus has said that if we are His sheep then we hear Him. So it stands to reason that if we hear Him, then we should also recognize Him when He is trying to get our attention. Sheep are very loyal when they have a consistent voice of a shepherd to guide them. Because the sheep recognize the shepherd's voice, they follow and remain with him.

As God's children we learn in a similar way. We have to remain in the pasture that our Father has chosen for us. When we are born again, literally, everything is made new. We are not the same person that we were before we accepted Jesus Christ. This new birth is intentional by God and forces us out of the way of sin into the way of righteousness. Because our minds always follow behind the work of the Holy Spirit, we have to learn to recognize God.

We often marvel at the stories we read in Scripture as how God led the Israelites and how He performed great miracles on their behalf through His chosen leaders. We must realize that those leaders didn't have an easy time getting to know Him. In our natural way of thinking, the Father will often do things that may confuse us. The truth is that our Father is trying to confound us so that we will get to where we rely on the way He does things. As we rely on Him, our natural way of thinking begins to seek out a higher way of thinking, even as God thinks. In other words, the Father uses unconventional methods of doing things so that we may stop limiting Him with our natural minds. This can be very frustrating because we limit God and His power in our lives by thinking contrary to the way He acts. Becoming more familiar with Him and recognizing how He acts can resolve this.

> *"...And Moses said to God, Who am I, that I should go to Pharaoh and bring the Israelites out of Egypt? God said, I will surely be with you; and this shall be the sign to you that I have sent you; when you have brought the people out of Egypt, you shall serve God on this mountain [Horeb, or Sinai]. And Moses said to God, Behold, when I come to the Israelites and say to them, The God of your fathers has sent me to you, and they say to me, What is His name? What shall I say to them? And God said to Moses, I AM WHO I AM and WHAT I AM, and I WILL BE WHAT I WILL BE; and He said, You shall say this to the Israelites, I AM has sent me to you! God said also to Moses, This shall you say to the Israelites, The Lord, the God of your fathers, of Abraham, of Isaac, and of Jacob, has sent me to you! This is My name forever, and by this name I am to be remembered to all generations."* EXODUS 3:11–15

We can see in the example of Moses' first encounter with God that he did not know Him. Just because we may experience a supernatural event or encounter does not mean that we know God. It simply means that we may have had an encounter with God. As we grow to recognize God, these encounters may become more frequent.

We do not seek God in order to see supernatural occurrences, although sometimes we may seek Him as the result of such encounters. Signs and wonders do not necessarily better acquaint us with God. It is as it says; 'signs and wonders' make us wonder. A mind that wonders will eventually wander away from what the Father intends unless He is being revealed in the process of supernatural encounters.

We can also see in his first encounter with God that Moses is very frightened and brought to great feelings of inadequacy. As our Father reveals Himself, these are the feelings that we often have. However, as we grow in confidence in His presence, we realize that there is no need to have tormenting fear. As we grow to know the Father, we recognize more love than fear. The true fear of the Lord is that which brings us wisdom. We grow to know what God is like and what He desires. We know how much He loves us and that everything He does is motivated by love. As we grow in this wisdom that comes from the fear of the Lord, we also have faith in God to know that He means us no harm and that knowledge causes us to obey Him without question. When I say that we obey the Father without question, I do not mean that we never ask Him questions. In fact, the Father often requires us to ask Him questions so that in His answers we know Him better as well as learn to think the way that He thinks. Our minds are often confused in recognizing the truth, especially since Satan has caused there to be a mixture of truth and error in our minds and hearts through his deception. However, communion with our Father will put this tendency to sway back and forth to rest.

We see that God has given Moses His Name and He told Moses Who He is and is now sending him to Egypt to deliver the Israelites. God knew that Moses would want further proof of Him being God. At the same time, it is through consistent inter-action with God, especially in our infant stage, that we have the ability to know His voice and follow Him closely. The presence of the Holy Spirit within our hearts is intended to give us revelation about God. In other words, because He is a real Person, He is able to speak or give the Father's thoughts to us. As we listen to the Holy Spirit more and more, we recognize that He speaks independently of us yet gives us the ability to be dependent upon the Father at the same time. He is separate from us and yet a part of us. He lives within us and influences us so that we may know the Father the way that He intends to be known.

Oftentimes we want to limit the Holy Spirit by trying to force Him to quote Scriptures. But in truth, the Holy Spirit is the One Who gave birth to the Scriptures. While the Holy Spirit may not quote passages of Scripture from any known transla-tions, although He can, He'd rather communicate God's thoughts so that we may hear them as the Father intended.

"...Every Scripture is God-breathed (given by His inspiration) and profitable for instruction, for reproof and conviction of sin, for correction of error and discipline in obedience, [and] for training in righteousness (in holy living, in conformity to God's will in thought, purpose, and action)..." 2 TIMOTHY 3:16

"...And you have not His word (His thought) living in your hearts, because you do not believe and adhere to and trust in and rely

on Him Whom He has sent. [That is why you do not keep His
message living in you, because you do not believe in the Messenger
Whom He has sent.]" JOHN 5:38

If a Christian desires to hear from the Father, he or she will
recognize God's thoughts or His voice through spoken or written Scripture. It is wise to know that if the Father is calling us to
do something, He gives us proof or some initial sign. However,
once our Father has revealed Himself, the important thing is that
we move forward in faith. When our heavenly Father communicates with us, He lays a solid and strong foundation so that we
may know Him. It is not always through memorizing Scripture
that we recognize our Father. Because the circumstances that we
live in often confound us concerning our interpretation of Scripture, our Father walks with us in the Person of the Holy Spirit.
We are actually being led by a Person and not altogether by what
we remember from Scriptures, although retaining Scripture to
memory is very important. The Holy Spirit makes our walk relat-
able. He causes us to see Jesus as a Person and not as some his-
torical figure that we hope is still able to lead us. Before we can
grow into the person the Father wants us to become, we have to
deal with who we already are. Because we cannot forget all that
has happened before we knew Him, we must allow the Holy Spirit
to help us to be overcomers in the world. As we get to know the
Father through fellowship with the Holy Spirit, we become bold.
Through revelation, we know that we have been with God.

"...Now when they saw the boldness and unfettered eloquence
of Peter and John and perceived that they were unlearned and

untrained in the schools [common men with no educational advantages], they marveled; and they recognized that they had been with Jesus." ACTS 4:13

Whenever we are yielded and surrendered at Jesus' feet, we have an inner confidence especially in the midst of tests and trials. This is the same confidence that Jesus had in relating with our heavenly Father.

So, as we have already learned, God speaks about who we are while giving us the ability to grow into the person He wants us to become. He does this by putting a doorway of opportunity before us and giving us the ability to walk through that door with Himself. The difference between the doors that we choose and the ones that the Father chooses for us is that the Father is in control of what happens on the other side of that door. The responsibility of our lives rests with Him as a good Father.

Remember, when a baby comes into this world, he or she has to depend on his or her mother to survive. The infant has no ability to survive on his or her own.

The Father positions Himself so that we may know the road that He has chosen for us and why He shows concern for us as we walk that pathway. It is very difficult for a foreigner who has no experience in the ways of a certain country to get by easily. In the same way, we must become and remain spiritually sensitive to God as born-again believers in Christ. When we are born again, we are absolutely new creatures in our Father. While we may be familiar with the world from what we learned as unsaved and nonresponsive people to God, we must learn a new way to walk with Him. This process explains the new door He sets before us so that we may walk from one way of living into the life that He has chosen for us.

GIDEON AS AN EXAMPLE

"...Now the Angel of the Lord came and sat under the oak (terebinth) at Ophrah, which belonged to Joash the Abiezrite, and his son Gideon was beating wheat in the winepress to hide it from the Midianites. And the Angel of the Lord appeared to him and said to him, The Lord is with you, you mighty man of [fearless] courage. And Gideon said to him, O sir, if the Lord is with us, why is all this befallen us? And where are all His wondrous works of which our fathers told us, saying, did not the Lord bring us up from Egypt? But now the Lord has forsaken us and given us into the hand of Midian. The Lord turned to him and said, Go in this your might, and you shall save Israel from the hand of Midian. Have I not sent you? Gideon said to Him, Oh Lord, how can I deliver Israel? Behold, my clan is the poorest in Manasseh, and I am the least in my father's house. The Lord said to him, Surely I will be with you, and you shall smite the Midianites as one man."
JUDGES 6:11–13,16

We can see that Gideon was hiding from the Midianites, the enemies of Israel. What the Lord spoke to him seemed impossible regarding victory and deliverance from the Midianites. We must know that when God shows up, He plans to change things. Whatever He says is what is true from His perspective. The Father doesn't expect us to do the work on our own, but He does require us to obey what He tells us to do. Even though we may doubt our ability to do what the Father tells us, sometimes our faith remains at the "hint" level to accomplish what He says. Our Father is looking at the hint of faith and not the mountain of faith that we do not possess. The Father has given us all a measure of faith, but it is up to us how we use it. Our faith will grow as we see the Father's ability to do what He says.

There are times when we can sense a greater presence of God working within us to do what He has said. However, though we come into agreement to follow God emotionally, we still lack the courage sometimes to follow through. We are never alone when we are directly obeying a certain instruction from our Father. Although we may not see Him by any visible means, God keeps His word. Let us remember that even if the Father has to cause time to stop for our favor in obeying Him, He will do it. In the final outcome, we will know that God is our Father and that He is the God Who created everything. The Father has no equal.

"...But the Spirit of the Lord clothed Gideon with Himself and took possession of him..." JUDGES 6:34

"And Gideon said to God, if You will deliver Israel by my hand as You have said, Behold, I will put a fleece of wool on the threshing floor. If there is dew on the fleece only and it is dry on all the ground, then I shall know that You will deliver Israel by my hand, as You have said. And it was so, When he rose early next morning and squeezed the dew out of the fleece, he wrung from it a bowlful of water. And Gideon said to God, Let not your anger be kindled against me, and I will speak but this once. Let me make trial only this once with the fleece, I pray you; let it now be dry only upon the

fleece and upon all the ground let there be dew. And God did so that night, for it was dry on the fleece only, and there was dew on all the ground." JUDGES 6:36–40

Because Gideon has faith in himself and has become acquainted with God's power, he knows that God will do what He has said. As we obey the Lord and have the heart to honor Him, He doesn't mind our desire for a confirmation to carry out what He has said to us. However, it is insulting to God's Spirit when we continue to need visible signs before we obey Him. In truth, further proof or validity concerning what the Father has said only pushes us from the supernatural into the natural realm. Therefore, we begin to wonder if the Father has really spoken to us at all.

"...Then some of the scribes and Pharisees said to Him, Teacher, we desire to see a sign or miracle from You [proving that You are what You claim to be]. But He replied to them, An evil and adulterous generation (a generation morally unfaithful to God) seeks and demands a sign; but no sign shall be given to it except the sign of the prophet Jonah. For even as Jonah was three days and three nights in the belly of the sea monster, so will the Son of Man be three days and three nights in the heart of the earth." MATTHEW 12:38–40

Unless we are becoming progressively discerning of the thoughts of God, we cannot see that Jesus is speaking about what happens to us when He has risen from the grave. There was a divine process through which Jesus had to go through so that we might have the Person of God in the form of the Holy Spirit living within us. The Holy Spirit now lives inside of us and produces the signs and wonders that we need to see outwardly so that we may continue to obey the Father's commands. This means that the Holy Spirit speaks to and influences us as we obey Him. We see visible signs outwardly that confirm that we are the Father's children. However, we must remember that we do not see this kind of evidence unless we are actively obeying the Father. Signs and wonders follow those who not only believe God, but also obey Him. As we honor Him in obedience, we recognize God not through His voice alone, but through the demonstration of His power and personal revelation of Himself. Obedience is the only proof we need, for God will always show men who question us that He is alive in us and is for us.

6

Following God

"...And you shall [earnestly] remember all the way which the Lord your God led you these forty years in the wilderness, to humble you and to prove you, to know what was in your [mind and] heart, whether you would keep His commandments or not."
DEUTERONOMY 8:2

"...The Lord went before them by day in a pillar of cloud to lead them along the way and by night in a pillar of fire to give them light, that they might travel by day and by night. The pillar of cloud by day and the pillar of fire by night did not depart from before the people." *EXODUS 13:21,22*

"....And Moses swore on that day, Surely the land on which your feet have walked shall be an inheritance to you and your children always, because you have wholly followed the Lord my God."
JOSHUA 14:9

Many times we give up following the Lord because we say that it is too difficult. In truth, it is more difficult when we choose to go our own way. The Scriptures teach us that the way of the transgressor or the one who backs away from God is difficult. The simple truth is that we give up when we feel as if we have lost control. We try repeatedly to do what we feel is the right thing. When nothing happens, we either write God off or seek another means of help. Remember, it is not always because of sin that our Father doesn't answer. If we harden our hearts toward God, choosing to believe whatever we want, then our heavenly Father will not answer us. It is easier to hear God when we are angry and have the wrong attitude with the ability to humble ourselves rather than to insist before God that we are right in what we think without hearing any response or getting an explanation from Him.

A great nation of people came out of Egypt. God's desire was to make Israel a great nation and to give them their own land. God did this because He promised Abraham that He would make of him a great nation. However, the nation that our Father was speaking of was not a naturally responding group of people. Those who responded to Him did so by faith just as Abraham did. Abraham believed God even though the things God often spoke of didn't make sense.

We have to grow to know God before His voice and instructions begin to make sense. When we try to control what the Father says, we often feel that He is not with us. Remember, if we change or dilute anything the Father has said even to the slightest degree, it is not the Father, but comes from us. Our greatest sense of knowing that God is with us is through following His lead.

We are told to acknowledge God in all that we do. This is so we may see how God acts when we invite Him to engage with us. There is nothing too difficult for our Father to do. What once seemed impossible becomes possible through the eyes of faith. We must look back in the Old Testament and see how God did many things with His people Israel. No matter what He did, the people continued to fall back into their old way of doing things. We can see that what the people needed was a new heart. By this means, they could follow God without the factor of sin constantly contributing to their failure. God stepped in just as He always does to help His people. We must realize that when God intervenes, He does so for the long term. God wants us to genuinely understand that Emmanuel means "God is with us" and we see Him when we operate by faith.

As we have accepted Jesus Christ and believed that He is the Savior of this world, we have received the Holy Spirit within us. Sadly, many of us still operate in life without any influence from the Holy Spirit except for what we might consider an answered prayer every now and then. If we knew the Holy Spirit's power to lead and guide us in this life, then we would practice a more genuine surrender to His leadership so that we might see our Father more clearly. In order for us to follow the Father, we must have the means to do so. Religion complicates the simplicity of the Gospel. There are too many rules in religion for it to be comfortable and enjoyable. As we grow to know God intimately through the Holy Spirit's presence, we see how He makes our lives more livable and enjoyable. Without the Holy Spirit's guidance, we cannot follow His lead into salvation. When I say salvation, I do not mean the salvation of the saving of our souls from eternal judgment alone, but rather, the salvation that pertains to our personal destiny from God. Before we were ever born, the Lord already knew us and prepared works for us to do well ahead of our coming to Him. It is our responsibility to walk with God, to follow Him so that we may better understand why we are in the world, and to enjoy Him in this process.

There will be difficulties in learning to know and obey God because our natural tendency is to do things on our own. We believe God wants to control and to keep things from us that we enjoy in our lives. We must experience discipline from God so that we know what He has freely prepared for us to enjoy in this life.

> *"...And I will give them one heart [a new heart] and I will put a new spirit within them; and I will take the stony [unnaturally hardened] heart out of their flesh, and will give them a heart of flesh [sensitive and responsive to the touch of their God], that they may walk in My statutes and keep My ordinances, and do them. And they shall be My people, and I will be their God."*
> ***EZEKIEL 11:19–20***

The problem with our hearts is that they are unresponsive to God before rebirth. We cannot expect something that is dead and not responding to obey the Father. Before we are born again by God's Spirit within, we are dead to God. We cannot respond to Him because we are spiritually dead because of sin. However, once our sins have been forgiven, we are then able to receive God's thoughts because forgiveness brings with it tenderheartedness. We are then able through the forgiveness of our sins to see how good our Father is. The Scriptures say

"....But My servant Caleb, because he has a different spirit and has followed Me fully, I will bring into the land into which he went, and his descendants shall possess it." NUMBERS 14:24

In the Old Testament, the Holy Spirit did not live within men as He did after Jesus' return to heaven. The Holy Spirit came upon men to enable them to do what the Father was requiring of them. Not only did He give them the physical power but also caused signs and wonders to happen so those who saw them would be strengthened in their faith. But this spiritual endowment was not upon Caleb when he spoke of pursuing the Promised Land in spite of the giants who inhabited it. Caleb had already witnessed God's goodness and believed that the Father was well able to bring Israel into the land that He had promised. He had an excellent spirit in God's eyes because he believed what God had said concerning the Israelites and remembered how He had cared for them. Based upon the Father's reputation, Caleb made up his mind to trust Him. He said:

"...Caleb quieted the people before Moses, and said, Let us go up at once and possess it; we are well able to conquer it." NUMBERS 13:30

What was it that displeased God about the congregation of Israel that day? It was their unwillingness to believe that He was their God. Rather than accepting this truth by faith that God was fully able to bring them into the land, they looked at the giants and the obstacles already in the land.

Caleb's faith was not new to God. The Father had already established a relationship with Caleb years before. Obedience does not always come easily for us. By nature we are creatures who want to know why we are doing things. Instead of asking God why we 're doing something to obtain further wisdom and insight, we often ask in order to find out if what we are doing will be to our advantage or not.

Our rebellious attitude that accompanies our questioning authority is what gets us into trouble with our Father. There is nothing wrong with inquiring of authority out of respect or for reasons of clarification. However, to question authority in the form of disrespect and to usurp will get us into trouble with God. It is our attitude toward submission to authority that either allows the Father to reveal Himself in authority or keeps us from seeing His motives in the authority over us. We must bear in mind that even those in authority who are not good leaders are there by our Father's own hand. If we recognize authority, whether it is good or bad, and respect it, then we have also been given authority by God to compliment the established authority and not to challenge it.

We can see that Joshua and Caleb's report pleased God. However, the fear that captured the hearts of the congregation of Israel led to their disobedience. When the other scouts who went to spy out the Promised Land spoke to them, they said:

"...But his fellow scouts said, We are not able to go up against the people [of Canaan], for they are stronger than we are. So they brought the Israelites an evil report of the land which they had scouted out, saying, The land through which we went to spy it out is a land that devours its inhabitants. And all the people that we saw in it are men of great stature. There we saw the Nephilim [or giants], the sons of Anak, who come from the giants; and we were in our own sight as grasshoppers, and so we were in their sight."
NUMBERS 13:31–33

Whenever we take our eyes off of God or forget how He has revealed Himself to us in the past, we become shortsighted. Whenever we are unable to see by faith what the Father has done and fall back into fear, we experience dread concerning the future. However, those who speak well of God's promises the way Caleb did begin to walk in God's love. It is impossible to walk by faith and not experience a growing love for God because faith and love work together. The sad thing is that because of the unbelief of Israel, the majority of them never entered into the Promised Land. We have learned that faith comes by hearing what is told to us by God or through what is preached to us from those who speak on His behalf. However, because someone is speaking by inspiration of the Holy Spirit does not mean that those who hear what is spoken will accept it by faith. The difference is that Israel had seen God's power and intervention and still feared that He would not bring them out of the wilderness which led to great trouble for them.

"...So we see that they were not able to enter [into His rest], because of their unwillingness to adhere to and trust in and rely on God [unbelief had shut them out]." HEBREWS 3:19

"...Therefore, as the Holy Spirit says: Today, if you will hear His voice, Do not harden your hearts, as [happened] in the rebellion [of Israel] and their provocation and embitterment [of Me] in the day of testing in the wilderness, where your fathers tried [My patience] and tested [My forbearance] and found I stood their test, and they saw My works for forty years, and so I was provoked (displeased and sorely grieved) with that generation, and said, They always err and are led astray in their hearts, and they have not perceived or recognized My ways and become progressively better and more experimentally and intimately acquainted with them. Accordingly, I swore in My wrath and indignation, They shall not enter into My rest." HEBREWS 3:7–11

We can see that how the Father responded to the Israelites' unbelief and His response to our unbelief and lack of faith is the same. We may say that God is merciful and is willing to work with us, but God was merciful to the Israelites as well. They never took advantage of it so that they could inherit what our Father promised them. Today we have this written report in Scripture. We must not deceive ourselves into thinking that we will experience different results if we harden ourselves to God's promises and instructions. We will still fail to meet the mark and not enter into the rest from God that comes through obedience.

Remember how God led Israel by His cloud and by fire so that they could clearly see Him? His Presence never left them because it was visible. Today, we follow our heavenly Father by faith in His Word. By doing so, we do not need a visible cloud or fire. We are led by His voice and the inner witness in our spirits that tell us that we are following our Father for the sole purpose of getting to know Him better.

> *"...But to as many as did receive and welcome Him, He gave the authority (power, privilege, right) to become the children of God, that is, to those who believe in (adhere to, trust in, and rely on) His name." JOHN 1:12*

7

Surrender

"...Behold, I go forward [and to the east], but He is not there; I go backward [and to the west], but I cannot perceive Him; On the left hand [and to the north] where He works [I seek Him], but I cannot behold Him; He turns Himself to the right hand [and to the south], but I cannot see Him." JOB 23:8–9

As we see, Job continues to suffer and go through hardship at the hand of Satan. Job, like us, looked for reasons behind this suffering. In his heart and mind he knows that he has done the right thing so that God will be pleased with him. Although Job has offered sacrifices for himself and his family, evil has come upon him. Job looks for God in this entire situation, but cannot find Him.

During such times it can be very difficult when we are going through things in our lives that we do not understand, especially when we have obeyed God. Even though we are Christians, difficult things will still happen to us. Satan hates us and we become easy targets for him when our efforts to please God are out of obligation or to be good. If we are trying to be good because we believe God wants us to, then this is self-effort. Our goodness and righteousness doesn't come from self-effort, but comes as a result of what Jesus has done on the cross which totally pleased God as the First-Born Son back from the dead. It is not wrong to want to please God or to do things sacrificially for Him. However, if our efforts are based upon what will happen to us if we do not, then we begin to slip from faith into fear. God is faithful to us, even when we do things that do not merit His faithfulness in our own eyes. If we see God as a Father Who cannot be pleased with us unless we function a certain way, then we are missing the point of faith. Faith is what pleases God because it reveals to us what is really in our hearts toward God. Having faith in Him and relying on Him alone for faithful living causes us to know how to live. We no longer function out of obligation to please God, but we fellowship with Him out of love. We see that faith causes us to change but doesn't change God's heart toward us.

We are told that without faith it is impossible to please God. We must understand that God doesn't punish us for not living by faith. If we are not living by faith as Christians, this means that there is a self-effort system that we have adopted other than the one that the Father has set in place. Once we accept Jesus Christ as our Savior, there is an inborn desire to please God. This desire comes from God's Spirit Who is now in us and Who leads us into fellowship with Him. In fact, the Holy Spirit's cry within our hearts is "Father, Father!"

"...For [the Spirit which] you have now received [is] not a spirit of slavery to put you once more in bondage to fear, but you have received the Spirit of adoption [the Spirit producing sonship] in [the bliss of] we cry Abba (Father)! Father!" ROMANS 8:15

This special presence of the Holy Spirit is intended to lead us to where our Father is. To be lost means to not know God or to not know the plans that He has for our lives. We cannot surrender to what we do not know or understand. The things we do not know about God are hidden from us only because we cannot see them in the natural mind. When I say natural mind, I am not talking about the functioning of the brain. When I speak of natural thinking or the natural mind, I am speaking of our minds the way they are without the Holy Spirit's influence. The Holy Spirit not only convicts us of sin, but also convinces us that we are no longer habitual sinners. Without having the Person of the Holy Spirit functioning within our hearts and minds, we cannot recognize God or accept the truth that God wants us to know about Him. The truth about God remains hidden from our minds. What our minds cannot see, our physical eyes will have trouble focusing on as well. Faith in God is created by the Holy Spirit and gives us the ability to come to God. This coming to God is more than just being saved from hell. It is coming into a relationship with God where He can reveal Himself to us as Father which means "Affectionate" One. As long as we believe that our own efforts cause us to be good with God or bring us into right standing with God, we will continue to struggle to know God. Because of this fresh sense of forgiveness and righteousness born in us through the Spirit, the good deeds that we perform are carried out as we participate with Him. So we see, the Holy Spirit cries, "Father, Father," which literally means, "Where is my Father?" And leads us to Him. This outcry of the Holy Spirit's voice within our hearts is intended to bring us into constant fellowship with God. Our constant fellowship sometimes becomes estranged as far as hearing God speak to us or feeling His presence. The Father subjects us to silence sometimes and to things that seem unfair because He is teaching us to depend solely on Him. In truth, it is a form of discipline. Sometimes we believe that we have to be told repeatedly how much God loves us. If this is the case, then God's love is not developing in our hearts as it should be. Love doesn't come without effort. Our Father continues to show us love that will always find its way back to the cross where it first began. God has always loved us. However, we cannot see it clearly or understand it until we really know why Jesus died and what we were saved from and for. We are not just saved and brought out of sin to go to heaven. We are saved so that we will enjoy a relationship with our Father in the earth now. Thus, we begin to understand, on this side of heaven, Who our Father is and who we are as a result of the cross of Christ!

> *"...And because you [really] are [His] sons, God has sent the [Holy] Spirit of His Son into our hearts, crying, Abba (Father)! Father! Therefore, you are no longer a slave (bond servant) but a son; and if a son, then [it follows that you are] an heir by the aid of God, through Christ."* **GALATIANS 4:6–7**

It is the Holy Spirit Who causes us to know the Father and not our self-effort. If we learn to surrender to the Holy Spirit, we also learn how to worship God properly and to give Him the glory for what He does. It is important that we know that what causes us to know Father is completely up to the Holy Spirit and not our personal self-effort. In truth, if we learn to surrender to the Holy Spirit, we also learn how to worship God properly and to give Him the glory for what He does. In obeying the Holy Spirit, we realize that it is not self-effort that pleases God, but the work we do as we participate in working closely with Him. As we work alongside the Holy Spirit, we see what we have in common with Jesus as a human being. By walking alongside the Holy Spirit, we learn how to live victoriously as human beings. We could ask ourselves how we can walk alongside someone we cannot see and the answer is easy to say, but not easily accomplished. The way is to surrender to God and to obey Him so that what we believe about Him we can actually see in reality. Our heavenly Father has hidden things for us and not so much from us. As we continue to walk in faith, He reveals what is not seen by the natural eye or understood by the natural mind. When something is revealed, it means that we now see what at one time we may have believed and not yet seen. When something is revealed, the search is over. We must understand that even though our heavenly Father reveals portions of His wisdom at a time, we do not simply take that portion of wisdom and make it a lifestyle. We accept and embrace what the Father has revealed to us and allow it to confirm within us that we are His children. This revelation that the Father gives to us through obedience is simply the life of faith. Accepting what the Father gives even though we may not readily understand it at first solidifies a stronger awareness and understanding of the foundation that He placed within us by His

Spirit. By doing so, we grow to know Him better based upon what He has revealed to us no matter how small the revelation.

> *"...The person who has My commands and keeps them is the one who [really] loves Me; and whoever [really] loves Me will be loved by My Father, and I [too] will love him and will show (reveal, manifest) Myself to him. [I will let Myself be clearly seen by him and make Myself real to him.]" JOHN 14:21*

We must learn to believe God so that we may obey Him. As we grow to obey God naturally, we begin to genuinely love Him. We grow to love Him through the way that He presents and represents Himself. This love deepens as we see that God is "affectionate" and is on our side. We must first learn to surrender to the Holy Spirit's presence and power so that He may reveal Who God is to our minds. The Holy Spirit will reveal God in a way that requires no self-effort, only that we participate with Him in this endeavor. At times the Holy Spirit will require us to do things that seem foolish so that our dependency will cease in trying to figure Him out. He reveals Himself so that we may know Him. Thus, the Holy Spirit enables us to relax and rest in His presence and causes a better understanding of how we are to seek the One Whom we have not intimately known up to this point. The Holy Spirit, if we allow Him, will reveal our Father to us so that we may begin to experience initial surrender.

8

Surrender in Bible Reading

"...You search and investigate and pore over the Scriptures diligently, because you suppose and trust that you have eternal life through them. And these [very Scriptures] testify about Me!" **JOHN 5:39**

"...I love those who love me, and those who seek me early and diligently shall find me." **PROVERBS 8:17**

I accepted Jesus Christ as my Savior when I was about thirteen years old. I did not know a lot about God at that time, but my mother talked about Him frequently. I would even find her praying sometimes and reading her Bible. Although I could not hear my mother speaking a single word when she prayed, I remember how passionately my mother would pray. The expression on her face and the body language that she displayed told me that she was praying. I remember a silent presence around her when she prayed and it was strong enough to let me know not to disturb her. If my mother could speak so passionately to the Lord, I knew that there was something that could be found in praying to Him. Although I did not know my heavenly Father then as personally as I do now, it was my mother's passion for Jesus that really gave me the incentive and desire to seek Him.

It wasn't until much later in my life that I began to feel the need for such a relationship. I cannot altogether remember what caused the desire in me to seek the Lord, but it had to do in part with what I sensed as eminent failure in my life. When I felt what seemed to be eminent failure, I had not finished college yet and did not know what I was going to do with my life. I had a talent to write and stage plays but when that faded before my eyes, it felt as if there was nothing else in which to invest my life. I felt lost and lonely. Even though I may have been sitting with my friends, I felt terribly alienated from them. Something was wrong and missing.

I now believe that these enhanced emotions of loneliness and a lack of direction in life is what we all experience one time or the other. Even those who have great careers oftentimes experience emotions that can seem uncontrollable as well as inconsolable. We all deal with our hurts and fears in different ways before we grow to know Jesus well. When we accept Jesus, we should depend on Him sharing His understanding heart so that we may know how to overcome what overcomes us in this world. Nowhere in Scripture does our Father promise us a life without problems. If that is being taught, we are hearing heresy and not the words of our Savior. We've already talked about how Jesus promised us that in the world we would have trouble and difficulty. The important thing is that we find Him in it. We cannot find our heavenly Father simply through searching for Him because we want to know about Him or even truths about Him. As Believers we must seek the Lord based upon what He has said about Himself. The Scriptures tell us to study in order to show ourselves approved unto God. This means that we are to engage passionately in the studying of God's Word, the Bible, but in that study we cannot forsake the searching for Christ in the Scriptures. Although we may study day and night using study guides to help us and listen to recorded messages of our favorite ministers, we cannot find God only in those things. Although they are helpful in leading us to the right door, it is up to us to surrender everything we know about God at that proper door and allow Him to reveal Himself to us.

The opening Scripture tells us that if we seek God, we will find Him when we seek Him with our whole hearts. The proper way to seek Him is based upon the initial way in which He reveals Himself. When we become born-again Christians, the Holy Spirit immediately comes to live within us. We have heard about being filled with the Holy Spirit. This means to be controlled by Him as He has taken hold of us and to allow His influence to teach us and show us our Father. How does the Holy Spirit do this? We must know that the Holy Spirit is God and God knows Himself. And since the Father knows Himself, He is quite capable of revealing Himself to us. The Holy Spirit is our guide in everything that pertains to God our Father. As we grow to know this, we can experience Him more in our everyday lives. The Holy Spirit is called the 'Comforter.' We must not limit the Holy Spirit's comfort to difficult or hard times for us, but we must allow Him to comfort us in the practices of life. In other words, the Holy Spirit can and will give us insight into problems we encounter each day, giving us peace so that we may know how to move forward or stand still. Whether or not God tells us what to do or not, the Holy Spirit can often bring comfort in the form of a person who knows what we need. And the Father will do this so we can see Him in the activity of the world as well as the activities we engage ourselves in the world.

The Scriptures say that God is with us. We do not know this as clearly as we should unless we allow the Holy Spirit to lead and guide us into the truth about God. The Holy Spirit will reveal to us the hidden things that the Father often wants to share with us so that our lives remain engaged in Him. The Father has extreme and responsive interest in whatever we go through and He shows it to us in everyday life. He enables us to breathe freely and to call upon Him based on not only how He has revealed Himself in biblical persons, but also how he reveals Himself to us now. God does not change. However, we must believe that as we study which means to look at and to ponder over the Scriptures, we see the Lamb more clearly. If we allow Him, the Holy Spirit reveals Jesus to us as a real-life Person Who is still with us.

We often struggle to renew our minds through Bible reading. If we would lay this responsibility at the Holy Spirit's feet, we'd find how He guides us into knowing God as we read His Word. Only the Holy Spirit can take the Scriptures and make them alive and relative to us. We can read the Scriptures and try to apply what happened to those written about in them. However, the Holy Spirit sets us up in a relationship with Himself so that we can see that the Scriptures are written for those who will live eternally beginning on this side of the grave. That is why we must begin learning what we have and who we are as the Father's children now.

There are many different voices that speak to us in the society in which we live. Some of those voices are in our churches telling us that God doesn't speak to us any more and that He has spoken His last words through the Scriptures. I could not disagree with this statement more. I believe that our heavenly Father has given us all the revelation we need through Jesus Christ, but there is revelation in the Scriptures that we have not yet seen. Our lack of searching for a living and breathing God keeps us just this side of knowing more of what He desires to reveal about Himself. Let's look at this passage of Scripture.

> *"...In many separate revelations [each of which set forth a portion of the Truth] and in different ways God spoke of old to [our] forefathers in and by the prophets, but in the last of these days He has spoken to us in [the person of a] Son, Whom He appointed Heir and lawful Owner of all things, also by and through Whom He created the worlds and the reaches of space and the ages of time [He made, produced, built, operated, and arranged them in order.]" HEBREWS 1:1–2*

Let it be settled. God has spoken finally through Jesus Christ His Son. However, there is much more that Jesus wants to reveal to us about Himself and about kingdom living and is speaking to us and communicating to us by the Holy Spirit. There is nothing new, dear friends, but there is that which has not been revealed to us in our seeking our Father. That is why those who seek the Lord more fervently, find out things about Him that others do not. The Apostle John tells us: "I am the disciple whom He loved." This means that John was the disciple to and through whom God's love was revealed. This does not mean that God loved John more than the other apostles. It means that John inquired deeply of Jesus while laying his head upon His breast, and received insight from Jesus that the others did not. It doesn't mean that what Jesus told John was not available to the others. It meant that John's closeness and developing love for Jesus 'drew' this out of Him. When all the others ran from Jesus, remember how John was the only disciple at the foot of the cross? John had learned that even though he may have been killed for being at the bottom of the cross, that there is no fear in love—dread does not exist—perfect love casts out all fear. When the other disciples were preoccupied with other things, John was preoccupied with Jesus. John had learned something about God's love that Jesus revealed and communicated to him. Thus, John had the emotional power to 'remain' with Jesus even in death.

Again, this does not mean that John was told something new, but was given insight into what was always available. The same thing applies to us as we allow the Holy Spirit to guide us in reading the Scriptures. We do not discover God through reading, but He is revealed. The revelation of Himself affirms much to us about ourselves and what we can do if we are no longer controlled by the power of tormenting fear which comes from Satan. In addition, we may know through the Holy Spirit's revealing Himself that we become freer in our minds and understanding God becomes easier. Since understanding comes easier to us with revelation about God, we mature in Him and become strong and stable. We walk out our faith rather than carrying it ourselves by believing things about God that may not be true.

I shared about how my passion grew as I saw how my mother simply adored God. However, I could tell earlier in my experience with God that He had something different for me to do. My mother was never a minister in a public venue. She was a wife and housekeeper who cared that her family knew about God. My mother never pushed God on any of us. Because of her close fellowship with the Father, I am sure she knew certain things would happen within her family in the future that she might not have been able to see happening at the time. I remember earlier in my walk with God how I believed that I heard Him speaking to me, but passed it off as me imagining things. My mother never taught me that God actually spoke to people. I just assumed He did once I began growing to know Him better. I will be very honest with you here. Hearing God is not necessarily a very popular subject among many Believers. Some of us believe as I said earlier, that our Father doesn't speak to us any more. Clearly, the Scriptures teach us about the communication of the Holy Spirit.

> *"...I have still many things to say to you, but you are not able to bear them or take them upon you or to grasp them now. But when He, the Spirit of Truth (the Truth-giving Spirit) comes, He will guide you into all the Truth (the whole, full Truth). For He will not speak His own message [on His own authority]; but He will tell whatever He hears [from the Father; He will give the message that has been given to Him], and He will announce and declare to you the things that are to come [that will happen in the future]. He will honor and glorify Me, because He will take of (receive, draw upon) what is Mine and will reveal (declare, disclose, transmit) it to you." JOHN 16:12–14*

So we can clearly see by this passage that the Holy Spirit has communicative abilities. He communicates our Father's thoughts to us so that we may know the Father better.

As I was growing to know God better, I remember sitting more than once and reading an old family King James Bible. Admittedly, the reading was very difficult. If some of the more modern versions of Scripture were around at that time, I didn't know it. As I was trying to read the Bible, there were several times that I heard a voice saying, "Listen to Me." I didn't know that it was God. The voice would sometimes speak to me even in the middle of my struggles to understand the King James language until I became frustrated. Even though I grew to dislike reading what I could not easily understand, the obligation that I felt in my heart to read the Bible remained. This has been the case of many Christians, including much older ones.

As time went by, I began to spend time alone simply listening to and becoming more acquainted with this voice. I remember that each time the voice spoke to me, I felt more of God's presence just as I felt during worship. I have always enjoyed worship. In fact, my first ministry was singing. Each time I sang, I felt God's presence which made singing all the more enjoyable. I also felt affirmation filling me which caused me to know that God loved me. However, I still did not quite understand that the Father wanted me to know Him more personally as His son. Intimacy must go beyond emotional feelings, even if the Holy Spirit inspires them.

As I struggled reading the Bible, I listened to the voice that I began to call "Lord." I know this is strange to some who may be reading this. I do not advocate at all listening to voices, but this was different. The voice always caused me to praise God more intimately and led me to read and study the Bible. The entire experience was mind blowing to say the least. It enabled me to pursue God and desire Him more than I ever had. I heard Him speak so clearly that He could actually tell me to go and talk with certain people or go to where certain sales were in stores. Soon afterward, I began to yield to the Father in most every situation. I simply learned to trust this inner voice to lead and guide me. In just simple Bible reading, I was never able to put the Scriptures together to the point that they would lead me. The voice, however, caused the words to become a present living message as if Jesus were speaking them to me directly. The more that I listened to the voice and read the Scriptures, I could see how the two were connected. Let me add that during these formative years of listening, I never felt that listening to God's voice was a substitute to reading the Bible. They worked together. In truth, the more I listened to the Father, the more He challenged me in every day life, even saying,

"There is so much more that I want to share with you and to teach you, but your unbelief stops Me. You have to believe that I am God—I am the Holy Spirit speaking to you." It could have not been more clearly spoken. Because I was learning to be led by Him, that comment made sense to me.

"....For all who are led by the Spirit of God are the sons of God."
ROMANS 8:14

Whether we know it or not, the Holy Spirit does try to convey this message to us when we are born again. However, if we are told that Father doesn't speak to us any more, we do not look for Him to speak in a more modern vernacular. The struggle comes when we read in the New Testament about the Holy Spirit and what Jesus says about how the Holy Spirit will communicate with us. If we read what Jesus said and still do not believe that the Holy Spirit speaks to us today, then Jesus' words could be confusing unless we take the initiative to seek Him based upon His words.

Shortly after the Holy Spirit spoke to me concerning teaching me more about what I was reading and a deeper meaning behind what the Father had spoken in Scripture, I began reading more frequently. I tried to find God in my reading and hoped that I would read the same things that He shared with me when I was listening to Him. I became more frustrated and a very strong presence of confusion came upon me. Regardless of how hard I tried, I could not make what the Father was speaking to me 'fit' into what I was reading in my Bible. One day He spoke to me and cleared up the confusion that I was experiencing.

"Why are you reading the Bible," He asked. Obviously I thought it was a foolish question because I was reading the Bible to get to know Him better or so I thought.

"To learn more about you," I said. Then moments later He said to me:

"No, you're not reading the Bible to learn more about Me. You're reading it to see if I am the One really speaking to you. That is why you are so confused. If you will give Me time to speak to you, I will make Myself clearer to you. I will make Myself known to you because I know that your love for Me and your search for Me are genuine. I want to reveal Myself to you."

As the truth of His words permeated my heart, a strong peace rose up within me, so deep that I almost fell asleep.

"I've always known that you were going to obey Me and follow after Me, and I want to lead you so that you will not be so frustrated. I am the Lord, Larry, and I am revealed. I choose to reveal Myself. You cannot discover Me through all of your studying. Keep your heart open and clear and I will reveal Myself. I will show you Myself the way that I am, and then our communication will be more enjoyable and intimate. Remember, I am revealed, not discovered."

"...You search and investigate and pore the Scriptures diligently, because you suppose and trust that you have eternal life through them. And these [very Scriptures] testify about Me!" JOHN: 5:39

It is a sad thing not to know the Person of the Holy Spirit. If we are to study the Scriptures, it is because we want to know God better. Unless we believe and accept the Holy Spirit as the One Who teaches us and leads us in our walk with God, then all of our studying is in vain and will only lead us to more unanswered questions. It is not necessarily answers to our questions that we should be preoccupied with, but rather that we know Christ intimately. Knowing Christ the way that the Father wants to reveal Him to us by the Holy Spirit settles issues in our hearts that we'll never settle unless we are willing to surrender to Him.

9

Surrender in Obedience

"...I cried with my whole heart; hear me, O Lord; I will keep Your statutes [I will hear, receive, love, and obey them]." **PSALM 119:145**

"...When the Lord called, Samuel! And he answered, Here I am. He ran to Eli and said, Here I am, for you called me. Eli said, I did not call you; lie down again. So he went and lay down." **1 SAMUEL 3:4–5**

"...Now Samuel did not yet know the Lord, and the word of the Lord was not yet revealed to him...And the Lord came and stood and called as at other times, Samuel! Samuel! Then Samuel answered, Speak, Lord, for Your servant is listening." **1 SAMUEL 3:7,10**

"...Then Mary said, Behold, I am the handmaiden of the Lord; let it be done to me according to what you have said." **LUKE 1:38**

We will continue to maintain the importance of cultivating a relationship with God from the beginning of new birth and building a track record with Him. This is so we will recognize Him when He begins to take us into other areas of experience with Him. It can be very difficult to follow the Father from reading the Bible alone. As the Holy Spirit reveals Him to us, we grow to see Him more clearly from experiencing Him in everyday life. Why is it important to obey God? Why is it important to surrender to someone or something we do not know? We see that as we obey the Father, He gives us insight and discernment that helps us to know His ways instinctively by the new nature. Because our minds have adjusted to the culture and do not permit us to recognize God, He determines what is the best way to reveal Himself to each of us. Regardless of how He reveals Himself to us individually, if we obey Him, we will remain in unity with each other.

For the sake of clarity, let me define the word surrender. I have not done so until now because I want us to understand that surrendering is a desire that the Father has for us as we grow to love Him rather than giving up because we feel that we should. As we grow to know the Father the way that He honestly is, then surrender will be a natural response to His love. According to Merriam-Webster online Dictionary, *surrender* means: the action of yielding or giving up the possession of something, especially into the power of another.

> *"And I will walk at liberty and at ease, for I have sought and inquired for [and desperately required] Your precepts."* **PSALM 119:45**

In Psalm 119:45, we see how fervently the Psalmist wanted to hear God's commands so that he might obey Him. There is a literal hunger and desire that develops in us as we seek the Lord and He reveals Himself to us personally. Nothing else satisfies this desire for God other than Himself. We are talking about an intimate relationship with God where He reveals Himself, not just keeping certain rules, regulations, or religious-regimented lifestyles. Because of a sense of thankfulness in our hearts, most of us begin our relationship with God trying to do what we believe will please Him. We want to please God because He has indeed forgiven us for our sins and has now taken us unto Himself. However, oftentimes we do not know that for which we have been saved. Most of us believe that we have been saved to die and go to heaven as well as avoid hell. Of course, not going to hell in any given situation is a very fond thought. However, God has interest in us now and not so much when we die. The Father's passion is that we are able to recognize Him now so that we can live victorious lives in front of those who do not know Him. Because of the revelation of Himself to us as Christians, He wants to have a genuine nation of people who call Him God and Father.

If we refrain from approaching God by faith as the Holy Spirit has led us to know Him, we will create our own rules and do what we feel God wants us to do, rather than obeying God with a sensitive heart. As we continue to obey God based upon His presence in our lives, faith becomes easier. We recognize the feelings that come with having faith. Faith is produced in us by God's words and words create feelings whether they are positive or negative.

We already know that Satan speaks lies to us that keep us in fear and estranged from intimacy with God. The Father speaks the truth about Himself to us which leads us out of fear into intimacy. Remember, we have already discussed that there is no fear in the love relationship that we have with our Father. That is why we will invite the Holy Spirit, even asking Him aloud, to join us and expect Him to do so, He will show up in various ways which convinces us that He is with us.

> "...And when He comes, He will convict and convince the world and bring demonstration to it about sin and about righteousness (uprightness of heart and right standing with God) and about judgment." JOHN 16:8

There is no way that we can come to God unless the Holy Spirit first convicts and convinces us, without condemnation that we are sinners who are alienated from the Father. Contact with God always comes with the sense of conviction. As we grow to know God, this conviction turns into the affirmation that we are truly growing to know Him. The Holy Spirit convicts and convinces us of our sin as well as our right living with our Father. As I mentioned earlier, this conviction remains in us as we listen to the voice of the Holy Spirit, maintain a sensitivity in and for His presence, and come into agreement with Him whether we understand Him or not. Later as we know that it is the Holy Spirit we are honoring, we will develop the ability to engage in conversation with Him and our times with Him will become more exciting. It is during these developing times with the Holy Spirit that we begin to enjoy and have fun as our Father's children. Jesus said this to His Father as He prayed in John 17:8:

> *"...For the [uttered] words that You gave Me I have given them; and they have received and accepted [them] and have come to know positively and in reality [to believe with absolute assurance] that I came forth from Your presence, and they have believed and are convinced that You did send Me." JOHN 17:8*

Undoubtedly, it is a wonderful thing to know that God did incredible and amazing things in the Old Testament. The Old Testament continues in the New Testament with the works of Jesus Christ His Son through our being born again because of His sacrifice on the cross and then moving forward to walk in salvation alongside Him. The Father spoke words to Jesus when He walked this earth. Laying down His deity to become one of us, Jesus listened to and for His Father so that He knew how to live and respond to God as a person going through exactly what we are. Imagine knowing where you came from while possessing all the power in the universe and then being subjected to what we are subjected to. It had to have been difficult for our Savior, but Jesus said that He had given us the words that He had received from our Father. Because we obey the message that is spoken to us from the Holy Spirit, the same words that Jesus spoke to the first disciples, we see how God is just as present today as He was then. God is with us just as He has said. We call Him Emmanuel.

Surrendering to God in any area becomes pleasant the more we grow to know Him, to understand Him, and to see that our Father wants us to succeed and to have fun with Him and each other. If we do not know our Father past what we believe He wants us to be based on what we know about Him or have learned about Him through study rather than through observation of Himself, we will eventually burn out and give up. We may possibly leave the community of Believers because we think there is nothing more for us. However, as we continue to surrender to the Father as He reveals Himself, we begin to understand why He has given certain instructions for us to obey. Rather than thinking we have to do certain things, we begin to see that we get to do certain things. These are the things that our Father has set in place for us personally, so that in obeying and honoring them, we get to see and know Him as He is. Surrender becomes a gracious act rather than an obligation.

IO

Surrender in Worship

"...For that which is known about God is evident to them and made plain in their inner consciousness, because God [Himself] has shown it to them, for ever since the creation of the world His invisible nature and attributes, that is, His eternal power and divinity, have been made intelligible and clearly discernible in and through the things that have been made (His handiworks). So [men] are without excuse [altogether without any defense or justification], because when they knew and recognized Him as God, they did not honor and glorify Him as God or give Him thanks." ROMANS 1:1–21A

"...You [Samaritans] do not know what you are worshiping [you worship what you do not comprehend]. We do know what we are worshiping [we worship what we have knowledge of and understand], for [after all] salvation comes from [among] the Jews. A time will come, however, indeed it is already here, when the true (genuine) worshipers will worship the Father in spirit

and in truth (reality); for the Father is seeking just such people as these as His worshipers. God is a Spirit (a spiritual Being) and those who worship Him must worship Him in spirit and in truth (reality)." JOHN 4:22–24

Those who began a relationship with Jesus several years ago and have continued to seek Him for more intimacy will tell you that they now worship Him based upon the revelation of Himself rather than the idea of who they believe He might be. When we begin our relationship with our Father as babies in the spirit, we do not know Him just as a newborn does not know everything abut his or her mother. We have to learn to know the Father through not only listening to and for His voice, but by obeying what He instructs us to do. Obedience and worship go hand in hand. Truth be told, we are not going to worship what we do not know. We can admire what we see for its pleasant appearance. We can give praise to someone for something well done, but worship requires a more intimate relationship. As God reveals Himself, He intends to give us insight into His true Self so that we may worship Him based upon what He has shown us about Himself.

We can see by the society that we live in that man was created by God to worship Him. However, we have replaced the true worship of God with other things. We preoccupy ourselves with things such as sports and entertainment. They are huge factors to consider when we speak about worship. Even before the current season is over, most fans are planning well in advance for the next season. We do this primarily because we are fans and have a vested interest in the teams we support. We spend thousands of dollars personally to either see them on television or sometimes more to go to the games. While there is nothing wrong with sports and entertainment, we must evaluate ourselves to see if these things take the place of worship and time that is due to God. If we are not going to worship the true God, then we will worship those things that He has created. Everything that the Father has created for us has been for our benefit. However, the abuse of anything can be enslaving. That is why we must learn to seek our heavenly Father for ourselves and know what He desires in worship.

Unless we have experienced worship and on going experiences of fresh revelations from God about Himself, our spiritual walk can become very tiring and potentially grow stagnant. We have to have God's Spirit refreshing us so that we may experience the spiritual life the way He intended. Recently, I told someone that we often associate having fun or enjoying ourselves with some activity as that makes us feel alive. From God's perspective, life is what comes from His Spirit being at home within us and producing life from the inside out. In other words, life with the Holy Spirit gives us such an experience with God that we do not need to look outwardly for satisfaction because we have found it within. The activities that we engage in outside of what we might consider spiritual are simply fringe benefits or gifts that the Father has given us also to enjoy.

Unless we learn to experience life from the Father's perspective, we will constantly look for some substitute to replace the Holy Spirit's presence with something that makes us feel better about life and ourselves. Birthed by the Holy Spirit, there is an inner awareness in us that tells us that we are supposed to be enjoying life more now than when we first got saved. Unless we continue to pursue and desire His instructions, this first-love experience we have with falling in love with Jesus is short lived. Because it is in following after Jesus and obeying His instructions that we learn that He is Who He says He is. Again, this produces visibility in our lives and we worship what we know and see. God becomes visible to us by faith. Oftentimes we complain that we cannot see God and that is why we have trust issues. However, the fault lies within us. We want God to submit to our way of doing things, to prove Himself to us by giving us signs and wonders and proof of His existence. If we are honest, the more visible evidence we require from God, the more we depend on what is seen rather than what the Father can present to us by faith. The faithful walk is filled with peace because those who live by faith know God and while we may not know all that God is doing, we can be confident that it is something good and to our favor. However, the life without consistent faith and reliance upon the Father is often filled with fear of what may or may not happen. The proof for us or the signs that lead us to wonder about God and finding Him is through the revelation that the Holy Spirit gives us about Him. Even when we do not see what we'd like to, He produces clear signs and evidence in us so that we may continue to have a fresh walk with our Father.

The Father has given us the ability to dream and to imagine. He wants us to use our minds because they are very creative to do good as well as evil things. However, we cannot do the works that the Father has given us to do or preordained that we should do unless He shows us how. The Father is not the One Who hinders us and keeps us from enjoying this life. In fact, He has given us everything in Christ Jesus even showing us in the Scriptures how we should live.

Jesus was a human being just like we are and sin affected Him just as it affects us. However, Jesus responded with the new nature and that is the nature of God's Spirit living within us also. It is through our surrender to the Father's presence that gives us the ability to overcome sin just like Jesus did. Because the Holy Spirit is now making us aware that we have overcome sin, the natural response should be to worship God. Worship includes the gratitude that we now have toward God for truly delivering us from our sins in Christ Jesus. The sad thing is that as we move past the strong first-love feelings we have about Jesus and try to establish our own righteousness with God, we struggle with feelings of sin because we have resorted back to self-effort. As we continue to move forward with Jesus, learning to recognize Him in our renewed hearts and minds, we worship Him based upon this growing visibility of God in our lives. We are thankful that He has delivered us from the power of sin so that we may enjoy life the way that He intended.

"...As you have therefore received Christ [even] Jesus the Lord, [so] walk (regulate your lives and conduct yourselves) in union with and conformity to Him. Have the roots [of your being] firmly and deeply planted [in Him, fixed and founded in Him], being continually built up in Him, becoming increasingly more confirmed and established in the faith, just as you were taught, and abounding and overflowing in it with thanksgiving."
COLOSSIANS 2:6–7

"...But, on the contrary, as the Scripture says, What eye has not seen and ear has not heard and has not entered into the heart of man, [all that] God has prepared (made and keeps ready) for those who love Him [who hold Him in affectionate reverence, promptly obeying Him and gratefully recognizing the benefits He has bestowed]. Yet to us God has unveiled and revealed them by and through His Spirit." 1 CORINTHIANS 2:9–10A

"...I had heard of You [only] by the hearing of the ear, but now my [spiritual] eye sees You." JOB 42:4

We struggle so hard to see, feel, touch, and put our hands on something. Nothing is wrong with this desire, but we cannot expect that which Father has made perfect by Himself to conform to what we want. It is simply not going to happen. Sometimes in the earlier stages of our walk with Father, He may cause us some profound exasperation. This is intended to get us out of the tendencies we have to try and control our own destiny. The Father is perfect in every way. He knows everything and is thinking about us. He knows what His plans are for us. Even if we had good days all the time, we'd not be able to match the plan that our Father has for us. Let us remember that our Father has created us and designed us perfectly after His Image, so His plans for us can be nothing less than perfect.

I realize that we all believe that we have certain plans for our lives and go after them diligently. We allow very few things if any to interfere with the fruition of those plans. However, none of us can honestly say that we will be satisfied completely by the end results of our own plans. The key here is following God in worship with everything that we have and even hope for. Our hope in the Father increases as we see how much He is for us and wants us to succeed. However, our tendency to want to be in control sometimes causes us to miss the mark. There is always redemption. We just simply need to ask for it. We learn to follow the Father mostly from trial and error. We do this in the beginning of our walk with Him because we are testing what is right and wrong as far as our understanding of the two. As we continue to believe God and to accept what He tells us, we begin to love His words and to believe that He is for us.

"...Great peace have they who love Your law; nothing shall offend them or make them stumble." PSALM 119:145

It is important that we do what Father tells us. We are to be doers of His words and not hearers who later disobey His instructions. The Father often gave His words to Israel but their rebellious hearts led them away from God. They were seeking another way to salvation but there is no other way than that which the Father has given to us through Jesus Christ.

Let us remember that we worship what we love, what we are acquainted with, and what we have an ongoing intimate relationship with. So shall it be with our Father as we yield ourselves to Him. As we honor, obey, and surrender to Him so that He may reveal Himself to us through obedience that we might learn to see Him and worship Him based upon what we know. Remember that Jesus told the Samaritan woman that the Jews worshiped what they knew, while the Samaritans worshiped the idea of God or what they thought God might be. Let us move past worshiping the idea of God and into an intimate relationship with Him, based upon the true knowledge of what He is like and what He desires. We will be pleasantly surprised seeing how easily it is to worship what we can look at through our now spiritual eyes that continue to widen and become more clearly focused as we faithfully look for and desire Jesus Christ.

II

Surrender of the Flesh

"....In the days of His flesh [Jesus]...." **HEBREWS 5:7A**

"....For God has done what the Law could not do, [its power] being weakened by the flesh [the entire nature of man without the Holy Spirit]." **ROMANS 8:3A**

"....Now the mind of the flesh [which is sense and reason without the Holy Spirit] is death...." **ROMANS 8:6A**

"....So then those who are living the life of the flesh [catering to the appetites and impulses of their carnal nature] cannot please or satisfy God, or be acceptable to Him." **ROMANS 8:8**

"But you are not living the life of the flesh, you are living the life of the Spirit, if the [Holy] Spirit of God [really] dwells within you [directs and controls you]." **ROMANS 8:9A**

If we are going to live victorious lives as maturing Christians, then we must maintain the sober attitude that Jesus was completely human as well as being completely God. We will do well to remember this in the struggles we go through in life. If we do not force our faith to work or try to make things happen without the Father, then the Holy Spirit will change us so that we may know how to live as Christians. Many of us do not know how to walk with God or to live the way He wants us to. This is because we do not know the difference between surrendering ourselves completely to Jesus and holding on to what we believe God wants us to be in this world. As we have shared, we have the tendency to try to be good because we now sense God's goodness within us through the Holy Spirit. While the Holy Spirit does not command us to follow certain rules to be good, His presence bids us to yield to Him so that we can learn how to walk as God's children. Jesus told us that He is indeed the way, the truth, and the life. This definition comes from a Person Who was actually alive and walking with God and doing what the Father instructed Him to do. We must increase in our knowledge of how Jesus learned to walk with God.

Let us understand that Jesus was a human being Who was affected by sin the same way that we are but did not think like a sinner. Even though He was assailed by the great passions that cause us to sin and the pressure to give in to sin, He did not. Jesus' primary power in His effort not to sin came from the Holy Spirit's power within. Jesus did not rely on will power alone, but He honored and obeyed the Holy Spirit so that He would not succumb to the nature of sin that beckoned His humanity.

"...For we do not have a High Priest Who is unable to understand and sympathize and have a shared feeling with our weaknesses and infirmities and liability to the assaults of temptation, but One Who has been tempted in every respect as we are, yet without sinning." HEBREWS 4:15

We should also note here that Jesus was in constant fellowship with our Father. He knew exactly where to turn during His most powerful times of being tempted by Satan. Jesus knew that His Father was alive within Himself as well as all around Him in everything He created. He knew where to look to find help in His time of trouble. And because Jesus has been tempted in every way as we have, even with the assistance of divine power within, He knows exactly how we feel. This is sometimes hard for us to accept because we struggle with seeing Jesus as a human being. Because we do not readily see Jesus as human, we find it hard to believe that He actually understands our weaknesses and hears us when we are being assailed by demonic attacks or struggling with varying temptations. We have proof in the Scriptures of how our dear Lord was tempted and accused by men of being from the devil. Jesus' success came from knowing Who He was inside because of His intimacy with God. God not only confirmed that Jesus was His Son inwardly by the Holy Spirit, but outwardly in all the things He did that gave visible proof to the truth that He was God's First-born Son raised from the dead. Jesus came to save us from our sins. He did not come to save us in our sins because He never did sin against the Father. As a result, Jesus defeated the power of sin that came from Satan through his deception of Adam and Eve. Jesus defeated Satan in the flesh. He did this by not listening to and giving in to the lies that Satan told Him and the pressures that came at Him to conform to what sin was compelling Him to do.

We must understand, dear ones, that Jesus knew the Scriptures. He studied the Scriptures as it was required of Him to know them. The Scriptures represented the thoughts of God. Jesus knew how His Father thought not just through reading the Scriptures about the Father, but He also recognized the Father's voice when He spoke to Him. The more we become familiar with the Scriptures, allowing them to reveal God's heart by the Holy Spirit, the more we begin to think like the Father's children. The more we think like God's children, the more we are able to receive, accept, and respond to His thoughts and perform holy actions when He speaks to us. This is called spirit-led living. We respond to the Holy Spirit and obey Him until we walk the way we were intended to walk before we ever sinned against God in the Garden of Eden.

We must understand that when we walk with our heavenly Father like Jesus did and even as others who came before Jesus, who although they sinned, represented God because of their faith in Him. In other words, God will always reveal or show who belongs to Him if faith and obedience are present in their lives. We cannot assume that living by faith is an easy task. We have so many things against us especially in the beginning stages of our walk. However, when we obey the Father and stop giving Him reasons why we cannot obey Him, He will reveal Himself in certain ways so that we are able to walk with Him by faith. Even then there are times when our Father Who speaks of the unseen and unknown will place within our hearts certain things that seem highly illogical. As we obey the Father, we will recognize His voice in the command. Because we are growing to know His voice along with learning how to follow His instructions, we will pay more attention to the voice that is commanding us. As a result, we praise God and worship Him because we are recognizing His voice in His commands even if they seem strange to us. Praise and worship are outward signs that we are recognizing the Father better and beginning to enjoy the way His Spirit feels to us as we worship. This direct response to Him through praise and worship better helps us to believe Him and follow His instructions. Worshiping God always strengthens and gives us the ability to believe Him more readily. It creates an atmosphere that fights away the hostile presence of Satan and gives room for us to honor God in spite of what Satan may do to hinder our obedience.

> *"....He did not weaken in faith when he considered the [utter] impotence of his own body, which was as good as dead because he was about a hundred years old, or [when he considered] the barrenness of Sarah's [deadened] womb. No unbelief or distrust made him waver (doubtingly question) concerning the promise of God, but he grew strong and was empowered by faith as he gave praise and glory to God, fully satisfied and assured that God was able and mighty to keep His word and to do what He had promised." ROMANS 4:19-20*

Abraham was called God's friend because he believed God. We know that he believed God because of what he did when God spoke to him—he simply obeyed. This does not mean that Abraham was perfect in his flesh. He sinned as we all do, but Abraham was perfect in his faith and obedience to God. Our surrendering in obedience to God's instructions makes us perfect in His eyes. The Father already knows that we do not habitually keep or obey the written law. We cannot do this. However, we can grow to love God in obedience to Him as we yield ourselves to obey the Holy Spirit. We gain revelation and the visibility of God through being expectant and assertive to His commands. Adam looked forward to spending time with God in the Garden until he and Eve sinned against the Father and fear entered into their hearts. Fear replaced the faith that came naturally and created a wall of difficulty and an impossibility of the same fellowship they had before they failed to obey God. However, we now have been able to return to the Father wholly through the work of Jesus Christ on the cross and His resurrection from the necessary death that was required by God for all sinners.

We have already shared that the feelings of sin remain with us even until we die and go on to be with our heavenly Father. When I say the feelings of sin, I mean the emotions, guilt, shame, and even condemnation that we sense in our souls even after accepting Jesus Christ as our Savior. These feelings can sometime be prevalent in our lives. We must continue to pursue Christ and the feelings or holy emotions that let us know that the Holy Spirit still lives within us, producing righteousness or what makes us right with God. We sense this harassment from what I will call the dead nature or that part of us that is sensitive to sin because sin entered into our physical bodies. That is why in the end, the Lord will give us new bodies which are fresh and alive and do not contain the old nature of the flesh. We will enjoy the new flesh. Although the Father will give us new bodies, I am not speaking about a flesh and blood body. I am speaking about the wholeness of our flesh as it has become spiritual, responding to God and doing what the Father requires. It is a returning to what once was: a flesh or spiritual nature that perfectly responds to God.

We can see in the Scriptures that we are not perfect in our flesh presently, but we do have One Who has delivered us from the overpowering of our fleshly nature at this present time. He is preparing us and giving us a growing taste of what it is like to be fully whole in Christ Jesus. Although we may sin occasionally, we are not habitual sinners as we once were because we are becoming more and more acquainted with and surrendering to the power of the Holy Spirit within.

> *"...We know that the Law is spiritual; but I am a creature of the flesh [carnal, unspiritual], having been sold into slavery under [the control of] sin. For I do not understand my own actions [I am baffled, bewildered]. I do not practice or accomplish what I wish, but I do the very thing that I loathe [which my moral instinct condemns]." ROMANS 7:14–15*

> *"....For I know that nothing good dwells within me, that is, in my flesh. I can will what is right, but I cannot perform it. [I have the intention and urge to do what is right, but no power to carry it out.] ROMANS 7:18*

> *"....For I endorse and delight in the Law of God in my inmost self [with my new nature], but I discern in my bodily members [in the sensitive appetites and wills of the flesh] a different law (rule of action) at war against the law of my mind (my reason)*

and making me a prisoner to the law of sin that dwells in my
bodily organs [in the sensitive appetites and wills of the flesh]. O
unhappy and pitiable and wretched man that I am! Who will
release and deliver me from [the shackles of] this body of death?
O thank God! [He will!] through Jesus Christ (the Anointed
One) our Lord! So then indeed I, of myself with the mind and
heart, serve the Law of God, but with the flesh the Law of sin."
ROMANS 7:22–25

So dear ones, we can see that there is a struggle coming out
of what we have grown use to and lived in. Even if we were born
physically moments ago, our sinful nature would be alive within
us and we would oppose God. Although we may be Christian
parents, our children will not be spiritual unless they come to
Christ. We come to God as individuals as God draws and leads
us. He also convicts and convinces us that we are sinners apart
from His holiness and righteousness. This is a war that continues
for the rest of our lives as the sinful nature tries to maintain and
control the greater or spiritual nature. However, this inner war
and struggle becomes less obvious and less powerful over us the
more we surrender daily to the Spirit of our Father.

"...In the days of His flesh [Jesus] offered up definite, special
petitions [for that which He not only wanted but needed] and
supplications with strong crying and tears to Him Who was
[always] able to save Him [out] from death, and He was heard
because of His reverence toward God [His godly fear, His piety,
in that He shrank from the horrors of separation from the bright
presence of the Father]." HEBREWS 5:7

It is so important that we recognize here that Jesus is a Son of His Father. We must see and feel the horror He went through as the First-born Son, the One Who knew no sin personally, but gave His life freely so that we may have life and enjoy living once again with our Father. Because of this, we do not have to be constantly controlled by the attacks of Satan and tossed to and fro by the lies that come from Satan to keep us confused and imprisoned within ourselves. Jesus literally commanded His soul to surrender to God by focusing on what He was sent into the world to do. With the Father's help, He accomplished His mission.

Dear ones, let us realize that we are not in this world alone. We have assistance from our Partner the Holy Spirit. If we choose to walk independently and in our own strength as Christians, we are abandoning the power that has been given to us so that we may know God intimately just as Jesus did. Yes, the temporary struggles that we have in this world may seem overwhelming at times, but we can either choose to be victims or overcomers as we see in our Savior, Jesus Christ. It would be wise for us to pray for the cultivation of a greater understanding of Who the Holy Spirit is and how He lives and instruct us today. We cannot imagine how much the Holy Spirit desires to reveal Himself so that we may know Him intimately. He also desires to reveal our Father to us Who is the One Whom we long for.

As we pray for the revelation of the Holy Spirit in our lives and wait on Him to do so, we will be refreshingly surprised at what He reveals and how profoundly He gives us the ability to live in the new flesh rather than continue to be enslaved to the old. Remember, it is a process; coming from the old and living in the new. It is well worth it as we see our minds changing and adapting to the revelation that comes from growing to know God as He is revealed to us.

12

⟨⟩

Surrender When Angry

"....When angry, do not sin; do not ever let your wrath (your exasperation, your fury or indignation) last until the sun goes down. Leave no [such] room or foothold for the devil [give no opportunity to him]." **EPHESIANS 4:26–27**

"....Understand [this], my beloved brethren. Let every man be quick to hear [a ready listener], slow to speak, slow to take offense and to get angry. For man's anger does not promote the righteousness God [wishes and requires]." **JAMES 1:19–20**

So, how is it that we are supposed to deal with our anger? Some have anger that can be very destructive and causes all kind of problems, including the destruction of good relationships. We must learn to master our anger. It is a good idea not to focus on being angry all are most of the time. However, it is very wise to get help if we are angry a good bit of the time without knowing why. To say that it is just the way the person is or to have someone put off getting help with anger management is not the right thing to do. We will be better off when we learn why we are angry and submit it to the Lord as well as others for help.

I can remember clearly hearing people say, 'You shouldn't get angry'. The Bible says that we are not supposed to be angry,' which is entirely untrue. Anger is a very healthy emotion which allows us to release frustration and stress that we encounter almost daily. As we grow to control our tempers we begin to see the value in controlling them. If a person can control his temper, he has a lot of control over his own tongue. We are told that the tongue no man can control. The Scriptures, however, tell us that the Holy Spirit can control our tongues from speaking things that are harmful. If we yield to Him, He can and will control our tongues. Too often we want to practice getting even with someone who says something harmful to us. This is the natural response. However, as we grow in our surrender to the Holy Spirit, we begin to think like Jesus thinks. We realize that whoever offends us has a reason and that reason may not always be as personally against us as we may think.

Sometimes life teaches us things that we have to unlearn as Believers. That is why we are focusing on surrendering ourselves to God entirely so that we may enjoy our emotions, even anger, when expressed properly which causes us to enjoy good mental health. But we must also consider that in the walk that we are growing to know with our heavenly Father, He may require us to do things that we do not understand. Because we feel trapped or do not understand why, our natural emotion is that of anger. There are even times when we may know clearly why the Father wants us to do certain things but we are angry regardless. Sometimes our Father may require us to go and apologize to someone who has done us wrong even though we may have not been personally responsible for what happened. It could be that the Lord wants us to take the responsibility, if any, for what we may have done so that peace and reconciliation may be restored to a brother or sister we've either harmed intentionally or said something that we really did not mean. We must understand that God is the God of peace and He wants us to live in peace with each other. If we are selfish, then walking in this peace will be very difficult. We must be delivered from our dependency upon self so that we may walk freely in the flowing love of the Holy Spirit. Self-centered living does not promote peace but anger especially when we cannot have our way in this world. Whether we believe it or not, we often try to force our way of doing things into our relationship with God. If we do, we will find our walk with Him or lack thereof becoming more frustrating. The Lord has already chosen a certain way for us to walk, and because that pathway is not what we would have chosen, it can cause a lot of inner turmoil.   Let us remember that when we are angry with God, it is very difficult to talk with Him. The key is being able to express our hearts to God by complaining to Him and not against Him.

Undoubtedly, we will get very angry with our Father when He changes courses in what seems to be midstream in our lives. He does this so that we may see clearly what is in our hearts either for or against Him. Anger sometimes works to our advantage especially if we can see how Satan is revealed in us when we get angry. This kind of revelation of Satan's attempt to make us angry so that we will not follow God enables us to better understand how tricky he is and how to better recognize him when he attacks. We must also note that this kind of anger will give us added energy to continue in our walk with God coming in the form of aggression to do what our Father desires.

> *"....The lot is cast into the lap, but the decision is wholly of the Lord [even the events that seem accidental are really ordered by Him]."*
> **PROVERBS 16:33**

> *"....Man's steps are ordered by the Lord. How then can a man understand his way?"* **PROVERBS 20:24**

We can be sure that when we obey God that everything will work according to His plan. Oftentimes our Father will frustrate our natural way of thinking not because He doesn't want us to think, but because He is trying to teach us how to think. By nature we avoid what controls us, especially if it seems to ensnare or take advantage of us with no visible return. We want to know whatever we give ourselves to produces some kind of visible return that is beneficial to us. With God, however, we do not always see the road clearly where He is taking us. This causes confusion and frustration which makes us believe that we are being deceived somehow. This is the case in the earlier stages of our walk in getting to know God. We must remember that we do not think the way that God thinks naturally. We are not born naturally from our mother's womb thinking like God. We are born into sin and as we grow older as children, we begin to demonstrate the same behavior as all those who do not know God. We must learn to obey God even though much of this comes out of frustration and anger.

It is important that we know that God will frustrate us so that we will get angry. If we are Christians, this awareness of anger will bother us and it will cause us to feel conviction from the Holy Spirit. So we must remember that the Holy Spirit does not convict us so that we can see where we are wrong and then condemn us for being wrong. Rather, He reveals to us where and how we are wrong so that we can be led out of what is wrong into what is right. And this has to do with every avenue of life. We are not intended to walk around angry and defeated in this world, but we are to subject ourselves to our heavenly Father and surrender to Him so that we may know how we are to live in this world as His dear children.

A CASE FOR ANGER

There are times when we can be so angry with God that we cannot hear Him. During those times, the Father is speaking to us so that we may avoid further harm to ourselves that could eventually lead to backsliding and completely missing out on His plans for our lives. As our Father, God does not like to see us hurting without a redemptive purpose. His permitted hurting in our lives is prescribed to cause us to experience righteousness in Him. This is so we may learn to master those things that keep us angry and emotionally disheveled.

Again, it is not wrong to be angry, we must be careful not to be harmful in our anger, even when we believe we are doing the Father's will and trying to convey that to others. We must be careful not to become angry when others do not seem to believe or accept what we believe the Father has put in us to do. The important thing is that we obey God and He will reveal to others in time what His will is. Sadly, we miss out on the Father's will when we delay obeying Him. Oftentimes our lack of obedience to God does not have anything to do with what we may have against Him. It may appear that our obedience to Him in certain areas does not immediately seem advantageous to us. Regardless of the reasons we have, disobedience is disobedience and it produces the same results.

Some years ago, I was planning to marry and I had a great feeling of love for my fiancé. I did not know that I was doing the wrong thing. Nothing was wrong with the woman I wanted to marry. The Father was trying to let me know that this wasn't the woman for me to marry. We may have strong feelings when we want to be in love and want what everyone around us has especially if it seems that our friends are all experiencing love or other things that they've desired in life.

God has plans for us all including marriage. If we wait on Him, that person will either come to us or the Father will cause us to be sent to that person. When we are walking with the Father, we walk into what He has planned for us. We do not have to take detours or short cuts because these can be very dangerous and set us back in life. It is important to realize that our Father is aware of what is going on in our lives and He has plans for us. His eye is upon us as He watches over and instructs us. For this reason, maintaining intimacy with God is crucial even when we are highly emotional.

When we are in love or simply infatuated, our emotions are high and as far as we are concerned, anything that speaks to the contrary has to be from the devil. How could we have such feelings of being in love and these feelings are not coming from God? Well, we must measure the love we believe we are feeling by the feelings we have for our First-love, which is for Jesus. If we are not willing to surrender any form of passion or love underneath this love, then something is wrong. If the person we are interested in marrying is the one whom the Lord has chosen, He will let us know. It is important to surrender our love to God because if we are unwilling to surrender our emotions to Him, we will be angry with Him, assuming He is trying to control us when in truth, He is trying to protect us. When we are wrong, our Father wants to correct us.

As I went along preparing to marry, the Lord continued to call out my name saying, 'This is not the woman you are to marry. She is not your wife.' I rebuked the Lord, thinking Him to be Satan. I said, 'Satan, I rebuke you.' And the Lord answered me saying, 'Larry, you know that I am not the devil. I'm trying to help you. If you do not listen to Me, you'll be hurt. I refused to listen to Him, allowing my infatuation to stay put and my anger to shield the Father out. Later when she broke off the engagement, I was truly hurt and suffered deeply from a broken heart. I could have avoided this if I had listened to the Father.

Of course, there are many ways in which we may become angry with God. He knows that we will get angry with Him and wants to teach us how to share our hearts with Him without anger so that we may become more reasonable. But unless we are willing to surrender and submit our hearts to Him for wisdom and insight, we have no ability to know His way or to learn how to live out our emotions in a healthy way. Our emotions are not meant to be hidden but to be expressed. Sadly, the world we live in often tells us how we are suppose to act, giving permission for some emotions to be seen and not for others, which can sometimes be the healthiest for us.

> *"....Regard not your handmaid as a wicked woman; for out of my great complaint and bitter provocation I have been speaking. Then Eli said, Go in peace, and may the God of Israel grant your petition which you have asked of Him." 1 SAMUEL 1:16,17A*

> *"....Evening and morning and at noon will I utter my complaint and moan and sigh, and He will hear my voice." PSALM 55:17*

> *"....I pour out my complaint before Him; I tell before Him my trouble. When my spirit was overwhelmed and fainted [throwing all its weight] upon me, then You knew my path..." PSALM 142:2A*

We see the ultimate act of surrender in our Savior Jesus Christ. We see everything that a son of God is suppose to be in His living example. Even in Jesus' most desperate moment before going to the cross, He was filled and embattled with all kind of horrible emotions including anger and depression. Jesus said this to the Father:

> *"...Then He said to them, My soul is very sad and deeply grieved, so that I am almost dying of sorrow. Stay here and keep awake and keep watch with Me. And going a little farther, He threw Himself upon the ground on His face and prayed saying, My Father, if it is possible, let this cup pass away from Me; nevertheless, not what I will [not what I desire], but as You will and desire." MATTHEW 26:38–39*

Is it possible to trust God the way that Jesus did? Only if we are getting to know Him better. Many of us are stuck in our own situations and unwilling to yield them to the Father so that He may teach us His way. Dear ones, unless the road we take is the one that the Father has chosen for us, He will not support us in our endeavor. We may feel and sense His grace in our lives. However, there is a difference between sensing the Father's help through grace and actually hearing instructions from Him and then being given the power from that same grace that enables us to do what the Father desires.

We cannot enjoy the feelings that come with faith and the peace that replaces hostile anger towards God and others if we are not willing to surrender our lives to the Father. It is through this surrender that we are to walk the walk just as Jesus did. Although we are not required to do what He did for the same reasons, that work has been completed and forever settled. However, as we walk with Jesus the way that the Holy Spirit ordains, we see what we have in common with those who are indeed born of the spiritual nature. We begin to take on the actions of Christ and the Body of Christ as we walk with Him. The understanding of this becomes clearer as we choose to surrender.

> "....Before I was afflicted I went astray, but now Your word do I keep [hearing, receiving, loving and obeying it]." **PSALM 119:67**

> "....[Not in your own strength] for it is God Who is all the while effectually at work in you [energizing and creating in you the power and desire], both to will and to work for His good pleasure and satisfaction and delight." **PHILIPPIANS 2:13**

13

Surrender When Afraid

"....What time I am afraid, I will have confidence in and put my trust and reliance in You." *PSALM 56:3*

"....The reverent and worshipful fear of the Lord is the beginning (the chief and choice part) of Wisdom, and the knowledge of the Holy One is insight and understanding." *PROVERBS 9:10*

"....There is no fear in love [dread does not exist], but full-grown (complete, perfect) love turns fear out of doors and expels every trace of terror! For fear brings with it the thought of punishment, and [so] he who is afraid has not reached the full maturity of love [is not yet grown into love's complete perfection]. We love Him, because He first loved us." *1 JOHN 4:18–19*

"....For the thing which I greatly fear comes upon me, and that of which I am afraid befalls me." *JOB 3:25*

Fear is a very powerful emotion and can be very tormenting especially in the hands of Satan who knows whether or not we are truly faithful to God. We must learn the true fear of the Lord as soon as we walk with the Father so that we can dismiss any false fear that we have in our hearts toward God. Satan will capitalize on anything he can in our lives that he can so that we will continue to feel estranged from God and cause us to believe that the Father is angry with us. If we feel that the Father is angry with us, then we will either avoid Him altogether or will hide what we believe is sin in our hearts during prayer or intimacy with God. We must know that nothing is hidden from God and we can speak with Him about anything, especially the things that trouble us. If we do not know what God thinks about a certain thing, we can ask Him and be certain that He will give us wisdom. Sometimes because we have unhealthy fear in our hearts concerning God, He cannot answer us right away. Knowledge is good but it can sometimes get in the way of what is true. While we may know something, it doesn't mean that what we know is the truth about God or ourselves from His perspective. Thus it is crucial to get to know God.

We can see that when Adam and Eve ate from the tree of the knowledge of good and evil in the Garden, they became afraid of God. One of the clearer signs that say we are afraid of God is when we are afraid to reveal our hearts to Him. This fear keeps us from being completely naked or exposed to God so that the light of His presence can reveal to us what is wrong and then walk us through it. As we experience this kind of communion and fellowship with God, we find that He is not angry with us, as Satan has caused us to believe. When Satan lied to us in the Garden, our view of God changed and there came a competitive spirit within us. If our minds are not renewed by God's Spirit, we fight against the true knowledge of God. While we may have knowledge as I mentioned earlier, it competes with the true knowledge that God reveals to us as He grooms us toward maturity.

It is our heavenly Father's responsibility to mature us and to cause us to grow up in our faith. However, it is our responsibility to yield to His love and affection for us so that we will grow up in the faith. And while we are maturing, Satan will often tell us lies which cause us to be afraid of what has happened to us in the world or in our life experiences. While we may not have a cringing and tormenting fear about everything that has happened to us, Satan is an opportunist and will paint vivid pictures in our minds of how what has happened to us will never be fixed. If we believe his lies, then we will always stay at an emotional arms length when it comes to having intimacy with our Father. We cannot enjoy God the way that He wants us to enjoy Him if our lives are filled with fear. True, some things happen in our lives that cause fear because all around us there are things to cause us to be afraid. However, the key is to not have fear living in our hearts, but faith especially in our relationship with God.

The fear of God is the beginning of wisdom. In other words, as we fear God out of holy reverence and awe, we become wise as to how to approach our Father and to have an intimate relationship with Him. Even so, in the beginning stages of intimacy with God, we will find that Satan targets what we are afraid of the most. We often focus our prayers on what we are afraid of rather than allowing the Father to give us faith that produces more faith that propels us forward in our understanding of Him. If we are not careful, we will find ourselves having faith in what we fear rather than having faith to be in God Who casts fear away from us. I am not speaking of healthy fears of things that can cause us physical or emotional harm. We should avoid things that can harm us because we know they can, rather, I am speaking of the fears that Satan puts in our hearts regarding our relationship with our Father.

For instance, we may have a problem with a certain sin or the fear that we might fall back into sin. Our Father's voice will reassure us that we can make it through whatever has held us back in the past. Since this is a process so that our emotions may recover from sinful behavior, Satan will often cause us to believe that we will never be able to walk without this sin haunting us. Satan's lies are based upon what has happened to us. If we believe him, then we will find ourselves constantly fighting what was and this will keep us from being able to see what the Father is planning and carrying out for us. Faith and fear do not agree or work together. If we put our faith in what we are afraid of, then it will seem as if our lives are in a vicious cycle. We will find it almost impossible to believe that we can ever escape the power of Satan's lies.

Some have often asked if Satan can read our minds. The truth of the matter is that Satan is the author of the lie and he is the first to ever tell a lie. When he lies, it is natural for him because his language is that of deception. While Satan cannot read our minds, he knows what tempts us and he uses this knowledge to tempt us even further to sin. He simply takes what already tempts us and blows it out of proportion in our minds and causes us to believe we are still living in sin even though we have only had a thought about sin. Since none of us want to habitually sin and if we are truly experiencing an ongoing life-changing relationship with God, we must continue to believe God. We must listen to Him so that the fear associated with Satan's lies will not carry us away from that intimacy with God. Satan's lies seem so real to us and are effective because our past is often more real to us than our future with Christ. We do not live in the past by faith because we can simply look back at our experiences and see what we did and what went wrong. However, we have to move forward by and in faith in Christ Jesus so that we may be recipients of the Father's plans and His visions for our lives that give us strength and power over Satan's lies. Our faith in Christ enables us to overcome the lies of Satan and to be victorious in life.

"....For whatever is born of God is victorious over the world; and this is the victory that conquers the world, even our faith. Who is it that is victorious over [that conquers] the world but he who believes that Jesus is the Son of God [who adheres to, trusts in, and relies on that fact]?" 1 JOHN 5:4–5

We must remember that simple religious things do not threaten Satan. Our rituals do not bother him even though he wants to receive worship and adoration. Satan wants to be God and will do whatever he can to enslave us in fear. However, let us remember that there is no fear in love. As we grow to know God better, we realize that issues in our hearts concerning fear are settled because we see that God is truly love. The way that our heavenly Father causes us to fall in love with Himself is not by giving us rules and regulations, but by speaking to us about ourselves and revealing to us in various ways how much He loves us. We must learn that the best way to get the Father to speak to us is to surrender our lives to Him especially in the areas of fear. Whatever causes us to be afraid is usually based upon a lack of knowledge and wisdom from God. Satan uses this lack of wisdom to keep us baited in tormenting fear that leads to dread. Having this kind of fear in our hearts prohibits vision and a sustaining view of the Father so that we may move forward. Whenever we fear greatly, we cannot move forward. Fear blocks and hides the vision that the Father has for us. As long as we are afraid, we feel more like slaves and not sons and daughters of our heavenly Father. As we grow to know our Father more clearly, we see that we have freedom. This freedom grows and grows and it sets our hearts free to know God better. As we grow in freedom, it is easier for the Father to speak to us about the fears that have tormented us the most. We realize that as the Father Is able to tell us the truth about what we are afraid of, our minds clear. It is much like receiving fresh oxygen after having been under water. When our Father speaks to those areas where Satan has held us captive and we believe Him, suddenly we are spiritually resuscitated.

"...For [the Spirit which] you have now received [is] not a spirit of slavery to put you once more in bondage to fear, but you have received the Spirit of adoption [the Spirit producing sonship] in [the bliss of] which we cry, Abba (Father)! Father! The Spirit Himself [thus] testifies together with our own spirit, [assuring us] that we are children of God." **ROMANS 8:15–16**

Satan hates all of us. Since we disobeyed God in the Garden of Eden, he claims us. He is unwilling that we should leave his kingdom as children of rebellion and become children of obedience to our Father. Even after we accept Jesus Christ as our Beloved Savior, Satan will do whatever he can to keep us in fear. Remember, dear ones, when we accept Jesus and become actual followers of God, we are spiritually transferred into our Father's kingdom. We no longer belong to Satan. He has nothing in us except what remains in us until our Father is able to produce salvation in us for Him and deliver us from the lies that Satan is able to use against us. Even so, we do not belong to Satan and in the process of leaving darkness and walking into the light of Jesus Christ, Satan's voice can seem very loud. Sadly, at one time we were not able to recognize Satan's voice as clearly as we do now. It is only because our Father has caused us to hear, know, and recognize His voice as His children that we are more aware of Satan's schemes against us. Having this kind of restored relationship with our Father through our dear Savior and Brother Jesus, we now have complete access to God. This kind of access to God is a threat to Satan especially if we are growing to know God better.

As we shared earlier, our rituals and religious practices do not threaten Satan. It is when we actually practice walking with God in the way that He has chosen that Satan becomes greatly upset. It is then that he releases demonic forces against us so that we may fear what might happen to us even causing us to believe that he has more power than our Heavenly Father. Satan is a showman. He likes to 'show off' and to do things that catch us off guard and cause fear. However, faith in God will always reveal Who the Master of Creation is and it is not Satan. So bear this in mind when Satan is attacking as we move forward in knowing Who our God and the Father truly is.

When I was a very young Christian, my greatest desire was to know God more. When I started walking with God, it was because He revealed Himself to me. He gave me insight into future things causing me to think the right way, and fear really lost its grip over me. We often have fear about where God will take us and where He will lead us in life. We believe that we should have control and say so over our destiny. In truth, we really do not know how to plan our lives, but God gives us His plan for our lives. His plan is not so we will have an occupation or some formal vocation, but so that we will know that our Father has set us in place. Purpose, identity, and individuality will come as the result of the Father placing us and not our doing this for ourselves. If we remain independent of God and try to make it on our own, we will never get to know God personally or how much He cares for and loves us. This lack of knowledge of the Holy will always keep us in fear, which is a dangerous place to be as a Christian in this world. We must know what a Christian is from the Father's definition, and this may be seen Scripturally, it cannot be seen in real life as far as the individual is concerned, unless we follow Jesus.

My joy grew more in God as I grew to know Him better and that He meant me no personal harm. This took a while because I was use to being let down, taken advantage of, and not knowing where to go in life. I began to see that I was lost (not knowing where God was or what He was working out for me) in life, so I took a risk by being in His Presence, listening to and for Him. I saw exactly how afraid I was when I was with Him because He always told me the truth, enabling me to see how fear had kept me from doing the things that He really wanted me to do. The Father has plans for all of us, but we cannot carry those plans out until we come to Him so that He may reveal them to us. Not everyone is called to be a public minister, but we are all called by God to be servants. We serve in various ways and this form of serving, which comes from the Father, brings definition to our often-undefined lives. It may seem that God is robbing us or taking something from us in these formative years, but as we continue to walk with and believe Him, we will see how our lives begin to take shape with vision and purpose. Satan doesn't want us to reach this place, so he does whatever the Father allows so that we may abort our purpose and destiny in this world.

I remember one great attack from Satan as I began to see that God had all power over him. Walking in the world without knowing that I had an intimate spiritual connection with God through Christ, I didn't really know how threatened Satan was by our growing knowledge of God. When we know the Father the way that He wants us to know Him, fear loses its dreadful power over us and Satan no long has control over us in that area. Freedom comes into our lives as the light of God enables the Father to speak more to us. Once fear is dismissed, faith and love are able to work more aggressively. The same way that fear has controlled us and caused us to be in bondage to it, faith and love move us forward in the knowledge of God. And as we are delivered more and more from Satan's kingdom, we truly see how much God has loved and cared for us all along.

There were times when Satan terrified me with fear, even causing me to believe that God did not have power to help or save me. I soon learned the difference between Satan's spirit and God's Spirit and presence. Bearing in mind that fear drives us from behind and faith and love lead us forward by a Savior Who reveals Himself in love so that we may be led by His voice. Even when He may not be speaking clearly to us or there are lengthy periods between when He does speak, our growing faith in Him lets us know that everything will be fine. We have peace rather than fear. There is no fear in this kind of loving relationship. When we are experiencing tormenting fear that causes us to cringe and to back away from the Father, let us remember that God is love and that He will cast the fear that Satan has put in us out of doors.

Yes, it will seem very difficult to release certain fears that have shaped our lives and our personalities for years. In other words, we have become what fear has defined us as. However, now that we have growing faith in Christ Jesus and are surrendering to Him, this fear is replaced with love. The way to perfect surrender in this area of fear is to acknowledge that it exists and to let the Father know that we are simply terrified about certain things that have happened in life and ask Him to give us faith in the place of this fear. We will find that as we participate with Him in the process, fear will lose its horrifying grip on us and faith will take place as well as a growing love and affection for God as we see how He hates what fear has done to us.

14

Surrender in Suffering

"...[You should] be exceedingly glad on this account, though now for a little while you may be distressed by trials and suffer temptations. So that [the genuineness] of your faith may be tested, [your faith] which is infinitely more precious than the perishable gold which is tested and purified by fire. [This proving of your faith is intended] to redound to [your] praise and glory and honor when Jesus Christ (the Messiah, the Anointed One) is revealed." *1 PETER 1:6–7*

"....So, since Christ suffered in the flesh for us, for you, arm yourselves with the same thought and purpose [patiently to suffer rather than fail to please God]. For whoever has suffered in the flesh [having the mind of Christ] is done with [intentional] sin [has stopped pleasing himself and the world, and pleases God], so that he can no longer spend the rest of his natural life living by [his] human appetites and desires, but [he lives] for what God wills." *1 PETER 4:1–2*

"...Although He was a Son, He learned [active, special] obedience through what He suffered, and [His completed experience] making Him perfectly [equipped], He became the Author and Source of eternal salvation to all those who give heed and obey Him."
HEBREWS 5:8

If I were to ask who wants to suffer for the Lord, very few would raise their hands if any at all. The truth is that none of us likes to suffer and no one wants to go through pain. However, sometimes pain and suffering are necessary for the healing process. We can see that pain and suffering were necessary for us in order to have salvation through Jesus Christ. Jesus suffered so that we would not have to endure eternal punishment and estrangement from God and have eternal life with our Father. But a price had to be paid for our sins. This is something that we should never forget and at the same time not feel condemned or guilty because of Jesus' suffering on the cross.

As our minds are renewed and we better understand Who our heavenly Father is, we see why it was necessary for blood to be shed or for someone to die so that our sins could be paid for. We had all sinned against God and in order for that to be reversed, someone who did not sin had to come into the earth and live as a man. He had to be tempted, tested, and tried just as we all are. He understood sin while never sinning once against the Father. This was the total package that was necessary for us to know our Father: the enduring pain, death, and resurrection of Jesus Christ, our Lord. We may look at what happened to Jesus and say that it was not fair for Him to go through what He went through to save us. However, Jesus understood the cost from the Father's perspective and what it would take to heal the sin problem so that we might be restored to Him.

Suffering unjustly never seems logical or fair, but Jesus endued the cross and all the unfairness that came with it. He had seen a spiritual vision from our Father before He ever came into the world. Sadly, many of us do not have a vision from God that we can see. It is not because our Father has not given us a vision that we can walk and live in after salvation. We simply choose to walk the same pathway we've always walked, hoping for different results. We even pray that God will bless the road that we take. However, we cannot expect our Father to bless anything that He has not given us to undertake.

As we walk the way that God has chosen, we see His compassion and grace along that path because it is the way that He has chosen. Suffering is part of that road that our Father has chosen and no matter how much we try to avoid suffering, it is going to come into our lives. The Father does not use suffering to punish us, but it is intended to purify and give us power over our fleshly nature. We have already defined the 'old' fleshly nature as the condition of man without God's Spirit living in him and influencing him. Jesus was born with God's Spirit in Him and never sinned; yet He suffered as the result of our sin.

The key for us to better understand how Jesus made it in the world without sin is to recognize how He maintained a holy and necessary bond of fellowship with His Father. Oftentimes, we ignore the Holy Spirit and go our own way and then end up in some terrible mess, expecting our Father to deliver us. While the Father in His compassion will help us, our goal in walking as Jesus walked is to learn how He walked—not as a sinner, but as a

Son of God. Hebrews 5:8 describes Jesus as a Son (with a capital S). This means that Jesus was indeed the Son of God and the first of many after His likeness. After His likeness means that we would be able to follow His example as sons of God as we learned how to yield to God's Spirit rather than relaxing in the flesh as we've been trained to do by Satan.

The difference between God's children and those who belong to Satan is the Spirit of God that leads us. Jesus was called a Son because He was the First-born Son of God Who actually obeyed the Father without fail. Unlike Adam, the first-born man who lived in the Garden, Jesus never obeyed Satan. Satan spoke to Jesus while He was in the world. Even in the midst of suffering, Satan was never able to get Jesus to abort His mission. Jesus learned how to obey the Father in suffering without sinning. Jesus could feel the oppression of sin through us and in the world, but He learned to obey the Father through the oppression and suffering that sin placed upon Him.

We must learn that suffering comes in this world and some of it is unfair and some of it is permitted to happen to us from God. I call divinely sent or inspired suffering from God as 'prescribed' suffering. Regardless of how suffering enters our lives, it is intended to teach us how to find and call out to God in the midst of it. Remember that we have already shared that Jesus had a redemptive vision beyond the cross: a promise beyond death that His Father had given Him and Jesus believed Him. We must also have a redemptive vision beyond our personal suffering in this world. If we do not, then suffering will eventually deplete our hope for a redemptive lifestyle with our Father now. The Scripture says:

"...In the days of His flesh [Jesus] offered up definite, special petitions [for that which He not only wanted but needed] and supplications with strong crying and tears to Him Who was [always] able to save Him [out] from death, and He was heard because of His reverence toward God [His godly fear, His piety, in that He shrank from the horrors of separation from the bright presence of the Father]." HEBREWS 5:7

Regardless of the tremendous suffering that Jesus endured, He cried out to our Father Who encouraged and gave Him whatever was needed so that He could complete the vision and mission that the Father required of Him. It is easier for us to complete the vision and mission that the Father gives us when we can see Him actively engaged with us so that we can succeed. However, if we do not see the Father actively engaged with us, we will soon lose heart and wonder where the Father is. Obviously, the natural tendency upon entering any test and suffering is to use natural effort of self will to make it through because not all suffering is divinely inspired, but suffering is suffering nonetheless. We often adopt the mind set that we can make it through certain suffering. However, when suffering is prolonged and our Father doesn't seem to be moving in our circumstances, suffering seems unfair. If we are honest, we can tell the difference in our prayers when we are going through difficult times. We think more about how to pray and what to say to the Father as we pray. However, as we surrender ourselves in the suffering process, we learn things about ourselves and about God that we would have not known before the suffering process began. If we are going through suffering the way that Jesus did, we learn that our Father is with us and gives us the grace to make it through and live victoriously above what sin desires of us. This is the same way that sin tried to force Jesus to conform. Rather than being conformed to what sin was trying to force Him to be, Jesus was transformed by what He knew about His Father and the vision that God gave Him.

It is important, dear ones, that we have a vision from God. We are in the world, but we are not of the world. We do not belong to the world even though the Father has given us every-thing we need to live in it. He has also given us as Believers His power through Jesus Christ so that we may know Him and how to live in His power in this world. Unfortunately, many of us do not know this power because we have not yet learned to surren-der in suffering.

We are told in 1 Peter 4:1: *"....For whoever has suffered in the flesh [having the mind of Christ] is done with [intentional] sin [has stopped pleasing himself and the world, and pleases God]..."*

How can this be? When we are suffering in our flesh, we are literally put in the position of making the decision whether we will obey God or whether we will do whatever is convenient for us. It is always wise whenever we are going through diffi-culty to pray and get the wisdom of God, but wisdom in suffering doesn't mean instantaneous deliverance. Wisdom could give us the ability to know what is going on, but a waiting process may be required before we actually make it through this process of suffering. Having the mind of Christ in suffering means that we think the same way Jesus did during the tests. It helps to have a vision from God in suffering because knowledge from God strengthens us.

Although He was God in the flesh, He laid down His deity and chose to live as a man and suffer as a man in everyday living just like we do. So the mind of Christ in suffering has to do with pressing past the natural tendency to do what we want to do which often leads us right back into sinful behavior. Rather, we seek our Father in this suffering and surrender our emotional or physical pain to Him and then wait for Him to answer. The surrendering of our pain to our Father takes much practice because as we have already said, no one likes to suffer. The more we fight to lay our lives in the arms of our Father we begin to see the benefit of suffering even if it doesn't seem like our faith is at work. The important thing is that our suffering leads us to our Father so that we may find strength from Him just as Jesus did. If we are sincerely honoring God in suffering, we will never be without reward. Again, this reward often accompanies the vision that we have from God before, during, and after we have suffered. Those who are faithful to God in suffering will often see the fulfillment of what the Father has shown them before it occurs. This is because surrender to the Holy Spirit provides insight into what comes next with God.

"...For he was [waiting expectantly and confidently] looking forward to the city which has fixed and firm foundations, whose Architect and Builder is God." HEBREWS 11:10

"He delivers the afflicted in their affliction and opens their ears [to His voice] in adversity." JOB 36:15

"....It is good for me that I have been afflicted, that I might learn Your statutes." **PSALM 119:71**

There are many uncomfortable emotions that we have as we are learning to walk with God as spirit-led Believers. Since we are giving control of our natural selves over to the Lord for our spiritual well being, we often feel afraid, confused, abandoned, lonely, and even have thoughts that we may be losing our minds, and conformity to what seems like spirit-led living seems more comfortable. But it is when we conform to something that is spiritually lifeless that we begin to dry up and even lose interest in what we consider "church life." We must remember that it is our heavenly Father Who is the life Giver and not the activities we often engage in that we believe produce life. The Father is our only source for spiritual life.

It is important to have relationships with older Christians especially those who are wise and who have learned some things about walking with God. The Scriptures speak of mature men of God as fathers and we need fathers as well as mothers in the faith who have suffered and have been tested. In those times of suffering and testing, these men and women have come to see Jesus more clearly in themselves and better understand this process. Even though we may really want to please God, we realize that it is not in our own ability or natural desire. We can only please the Father by taking the special road that He has chosen for us, for included along the pathway is the necessary conflict and suffering that causes us to know God as He wants to be known.

These divinely inspired sufferings teach us how to talk to God. Even our prayer times are lessened because we pray the truth to our Father and express ourselves out of our knowledge of Him rather than plead with Him to do something that may not be His will. The Father's will becomes clearer once we have suffered and even though we believe our dreams will make us happy in life, we give them up. As a result, this kind of behavior is prerequisite to us having a genuine vision from God. Once we see that the Father has a plan that brings peace, rest, confidence in Him, and delivers us from fear, we begin to rest in His care. We know that the power we need is within us by the Holy Spirit as we yield to Him so that He can do what He is called to do, and that is leading us in the way that the Father has chosen even when that means suffering.

We may look at the time that it takes to go through this suffering process and wonder how long we will have to endure it. We look at things from a finite point of view. Our Father is interested in us seeing things from His perspective which increases our ability to see much farther so that we may be sustained by what we know as He has revealed it to us. Suffering in the flesh provides what is necessary for us to see past the natural tendency of our minds. Suffering is part of the transformation that is necessary for us to hear, know, and see the Father the way that He desires. Without this kind of suffering prescribed by our Father, we cannot learn to obey Him exactly.

"...I am writing to you, fathers, because you have come to know (recognize, be aware of, and understand) Him Who [has existed] from the beginning." 1 JOHN 2:12A

"....For one is regarded favorably (is approved, acceptable, and thankworthy) if, as in the sight of God, he endures the pain of unjust suffering.... But if you bear patiently with suffering [which results] when you do right and that is undeserved, it is acceptable and pleasing to God.   For even to this were you called [it is inseparable from your vocation].   For Christ also suffered for you, leaving you [His personal] example, so that you should follow in His footsteps." 1 PETER 2:19A–20B,21

"And after you have suffered a little while, the God of all grace [Who imparts all blessing and favor], Who has called you to His [own] eternal glory in Christ Jesus, will Himself complete and make you what you ought to be, establish and ground you securely, and strengthen, and settle you." 1 PETER 5:10

15

Surrender in Life

"....For we do not have a High Priest Who is unable to understand and sympathize and have a shared feeling with our weaknesses and infirmities and liability to the assaults of temptation, but One Who has been tempted in every respect as we are, yet without sinning. Let us then fearlessly and confidently and boldly draw near to the throne of grace (the throne of God's unmerited favor to us sinners), that we may receive mercy [for our failures] and find grace to help in good time for every need [appropriate help and well-timed help, coming just when we need it]." HEBREWS 4:15–16

"....Therefore He is able also to save to the uttermost (completely, perfectly, finally, and for all time and eternity) those who come to God through Him, since He is always living to make petition to God and intercede with Him and intervene for them." HEBREWS 7:25

One of the hardest things that we will ever do as Believers in Christ is to surrender our lives to Jesus. This is not because Jesus is difficult to surrender to, but because we do not want to give up our lives. Sadly, if we do not pursue Jesus immediately after being born again by His Spirit, we will lose something. The best time to pursue our Father, in this newly born love in our hearts, is when we are newly saved and the freshness of His love is genuinely felt in our hearts. This is not the time to continue looking for God, as we were when we really did not have His help in this world and pursued Him based upon religious rules and what our minds told us. Unless God's Spirit draws and convicts us, we have no true investment in Jesus and He is the only way that we can know our heavenly Father. This pursuit of Jesus for the reason of knowing Who He is will lead us to know who we are and this citizenship we now have as our Father's children. Knowing Jesus enables us to know that pathway that our Father has chosen for us and that pathway is very similar to that which Jesus walked. It is a pathway of suffering, a pathway that very few take, but it is the pathway that our Father has chosen.

> "...Surely He has borne our griefs (sicknesses, weakness, and distresses) and carried our sorrows and pains [of punishment], yet we [ignorantly] considered Him stricken, smitten, and afflicted by God [as if with leprosy]. But He was wounded for our transgressions, He was bruised for our guilt and iniquities; the chastisement [needful to obtain] peace and well-being for us was upon Him, and with the stripes [that wounded] Him we are healed and made whole." ISAIAH 53:4–5

Our primary investment for our lives in this world should be to know Jesus. If we make it a necessity to seek Him, then we will better understand and know Him in His humanity. We often fail to realize that Jesus was a human being and believe that He was able to do what He did by sheer will power alone. We forget that He learned how to obey the Father in spite of sin by what He suffered. Jesus felt the effects of sin and how horrible the feelings are that pull and draw on us as we try with will power alone not to sin. However, Jesus forced Himself as a human being not to sin by yielding His own will to His Father. We can see how difficult this was as sin tried to take His life out of Him in the garden of Gethsemane. Even His friends lay asleep a short distance from Him when He needed them the most.

In Jesus, if we look carefully enough and are willing to open our eyes and see the truth clearly revealed by the Holy Spirit, we can see how He suffered for us and what He did in His suffering. If we see this great revelation of His humanity, then we know where to go for help and find assistance and assured help from our Father, the same way that Jesus did. We must remember, dear ones, that Jesus was a Son just as we are. He was God in the flesh. God lived in and possessed His flesh, but Jesus could have chosen to sin even as we choose to sin after knowing the truth about the Father through Him. Jesus did not sin. He refused to abandon what the Father had called Him to do in this earth and engaged in natural resistance against sin while receiving power from the Father to finish His mission.

"....So, since Christ suffered in the flesh for us, for you, arm yourselves with the same thought and purpose [patiently to suffer rather than fail to please God]." 1 PETER 4:1

Why so much suffering? Why so much hardship? Anyone who has genuinely tried to walk with God knows that sin doesn't give up easily. What Satan did to us by causing us to come out of agreement with God through sin has dealt us a deathblow that only Jesus can reverse. Because we believed Satan in the Garden, he feels that he has some investment in us and he does, but only until our Father delivers us through the blood of Jesus Christ. We must remember that blood is shed because life is in the blood and without the shedding of the blood of Jesus Who was our perfect Lamb; there is no forgiveness of sins. So rather than concentrate on the horrible things that happened to Jesus, we should focus on the ransom we have from the power of sin through the work of Jesus. Unless we can come to the point where we can be empathetic with Jesus' sufferings as a man and see the reason why it was necessary for Him to suffer, we will never be able to enjoy the benefits we have in Him for the release of sin.

The more we see the sufferings of Jesus from the view point of the Holy Spirit Who enabled Jesus to suffer manfully, the more we will run to Him for His aid in our current sufferings. As we find strength in the Holy Spirit and know the truth more from what He sees and reveals to us, the more we understand that sin loses its power over us as we experience divine sufferings that lead us out of sin and into the Father's arms. As we have already mentioned, no one likes to suffer and we plan around it and try to avoid it at all costs, however, some suffering is necessary. If we look for Him in our suffering, it teaches us where our Father can be found. This knowing where our Father can be found when we are suffering, will enable us to know how Jesus overcame suffering sin in His humanity. If we are gong to walk the way that Jesus walked as part of our vocation in this new nature we have in Christ, we must learn the way of surrendering to God in suffering.

> *"....Since, therefore, [these His] children share in flesh and blood [in the physical nature of human beings], He [Himself] in a similar manner partook of the same [nature], that by [going through] death He might bring to nought and make of no effect him who had the power of death—that is, the devil, and also that He might deliver and completely set free all those who through the [haunting] fear of death were held in bondage throughout the whole course of their lives." HEBREWS 2:14–15*

> *"....The reason the Son of God was made manifest (visible) was to undo (destroy, loosen, and dissolve) the works the devil [has done]." 1 JOHN 3:8B*

The Lord has often reminded me as I grow older how it was necessary for me to suffer if I was going to walk with Him. Of course, it didn't make sense to me when I was younger. It didn't seem fair to suffer and to find myself being attacked by Satan so often. But the truth of the matter is that Satan attacked me because I was growing to know God better. At the time I was going through the suffering, I did not realize that it was causing me to be very raw and honest with God. What was in my heart—

accusations against God, cursing, disrespect, and ignorance of Who God is—became evident during the times of suffering. I knew that suffering had played its part in my life when I came to my senses and apologized to God.

We know that God has been able to reveal Himself to us when we have suffered. We see Him more clearly and realize that sin has blinded us and caused us to think only of ourselves. We want to be delivered from our present pain. After all, since Jesus suffered for all of our sins, why should we have to? It is true that Jesus suffered for us, but our suffering puts us in the place where we can see what we have in common with Jesus as a human being bearing our sin, not His. The suffering that we endure is intended to teach us where our Father can be found so that He will reveal Himself. In this way, we can see Him clearly and worship Him out of the revelation of Himself to us as we surrender in our suffering.

"...My son, do not think lightly or scorn to submit to the correction and discipline of the Lord, nor lose courage and give up and faint when you are reproved or corrected by Him; for the Lord corrects and disciplines everyone whom He loves, and He punishes, even scourges, every son whom He accepts and welcomes to His heart and cherishes. You must submit to and endure [correction] for discipline; God is dealing with you as with sons."
HEBREWS 12:5B–7A

"...For the time being no discipline brings joy, but seems grievous and painful; but afterwards it yields a peaceable fruit of righteousness to those who have been trained by it [a harvest of

fruit which consists in righteousness—in conformity to God's will in purpose, thought, and action, resulting in right living and right standing with God]." HEBREWS 12:11

".... I had heard of You [only] by the hearing of the ear, but now my [spiritual] eye sees You. Therefore I loathe [my words] and abhor myself and repent in dust and ashes." JOB 42:5–6

The suffering that we go through as Believers will indeed lead us into places where we've never been, beckoning us to relinquish our lives and give control to the One Who knows us much better than we know ourselves. In this process of surrender, which can be very painful and even cause us to wonder if we are actually losing our minds, we begin to regain our minds. Our minds were intended to recognize the Father and to know the road that He has chosen for us in life. In this way, we may learn from Him how to find that way of life and to choose that way of life so that we may enjoy the Father in the world.

"The Lord is my Shepherd [to feed, guide, and shield me], I shall not lack...He refreshes and restores my life (my self)..." (PSALM 23:1,3A

Until we know the way that our Father has chosen for us we will continue to wander almost aimlessly in the earth. We cannot find the way of God on our own and in our ever-consuming self effort. However, as we surrender to Him so that the work of our flesh is clearly seen for what it is, we recognize that there is a better way and learn how to walk in that way. Once something has been revealed to us from God, we should cease looking for it or an alternative because the true way has come and replaces the counterfeit.

The purpose of our Father is to put to death the deeds and workings of the fleshly nature that has ruled and governed us all of our lives. And as we believe that Jesus is our Savior and move forward in Him, this vicious cycle of habitual sin is broken so that we may be able to grasp and understand what it means to be led by the Spirit Who has brought us to life. Unless there is death to our agreeing with and continuing to walk in the flesh, we will continue to be bound in sin and desire a way out when Jesus already afforded us this great blessing. However, surrender by faith to what is unknown and unseen is necessary to see this new way of life. Without dying to the old way of living and coming into the new way of life that Christ has given us, we cannot experience the power of the Holy Spirit that raised Jesus up from the dead. Once we die to sin and continue to experience life and salvation from the power of the Holy Spirit in us, we can continue to move forward in everyday living, where our minds can see more clearly that God is with us. This further produces the truth to us in visible form. Believing and obeying God will always produce visible results that He is with us.

> *"...For I through the Law [under the operation of the curse of the Law] have [in Christ's death for me] myself died to the Law and all the Law's demands upon me, so that I may [henceforth] live to and for God. I have been crucified with Christ, [in Him I have shared His crucifixion]; it is no longer I who live, but Christ (the Messiah) lives in me; and the life I now live in the body I live by*

faith in (by adherence to and reliance on and complete trust in) the Son of God Who loved me and gave Himself up for me."
GALATIANS 2:19–20

Let us continue to put into practice the surrendering of our hearts to Jesus regarding all that concerns us in life. Although He is the God of heaven, He has always conquered everything that is in the earth that held us bound at one time. Surrender is the key to knowing God more fully and growing to know His will more effectively so that it might be accomplished in us in this world. Remember, He has given us a certain pathway by which we are to walk. As we walk that pathway, we will encounter difficulty, but let us not grow tired and weary of what the Father has placed before us: His divine plan for our lives. Be encouraged as we walk with Him and see His plan revealed to us as we walk along the way. He has compassion for the way that He has chosen for us because it is the way that He has chosen. We would not have chosen it on our own.

"...But He knows the way that I take [He has concern for it, appreciates, and pays attention to it]. When He has tried me, I shall come forth as refined gold [pure and luminous]." **JOB 23:10**